Farm Food

Farm Food Volume I FALL & WINTER

Cookhouse Publishing
18409 Beall Road SW
Vashon, WA 98070
www.kurtwoodfarms.com

ISBN 9780999172308

Farm
Food

Volume One

FALL & WINTER

Text & photographs by

KURT TIMMERMEISTER

Recipes

Introduction.

This is neither a book nor a magazine; it is a serialized cookbook, if you will. Except that it isn't really a cookbook. Sure, there are recipes included. But *Farm Food* is more like a diary of my farm, illustrated with food and photographs.

Kurtwood Farms is a small commercial dairy farm on Vashon Island. We make cheese and ice cream, but mostly we just make food. There is an orchard and a garden and a flock of chickens and some hogs, along with a herd of cows producing remarkable milk.

My goal is to grow and produce as much of my own food as possible on these thirteen fertile acres. I try to buy just a few things at the store: organic cane sugar, wheat berries, green coffee beans from Honduras, rice, sea salt, and peppercorns. Sometimes I give in and buy a few other things: cinnamon sticks, whole nutmeg, oranges in the winter, and rice wine vinegar. I probably could make rice wine vinegar but I haven't figured out how yet. And soy sauce; I buy soy sauce. I want to say that the oranges are to ward off scurvy but mostly I just love them in the chill of winter. And olive oil, I have been talked into buying olive oil from time to time. But the rest I try to grow or make myself, and the stories and recipes in this first volume all take their ingredients—the plums and the pork chops and the butter and so on—from my farm. I want to show a very local cuisine, a way of cooking just from this bit of land.

It goes without saying that we eat well here. Only I and my dog live on the farm, but employees work here everyday, milking cows and making cheese. And friends come by for meals: small snacks for cheese tastings, casual dinners during the week, and larger feasts for holidays and summertime parties. There are always projects in the works: bread rising, plums drying, or vinegar curing.

Farm Food is a peek into life here on this farm. This first volume covers fall and winter on the farm and in the kitchen. A second volume will follow, describing the spring and summer months. I'll share with you a full life on this bit of ground: one that shows the wet, muddy months and the bright, endlessly hot weeks. The toughest days and the easiest days. And the pies and cakes, cocktails and pickles, and salads and roasts that make it all fabulous. And the biscuits. Gotta have biscuits, too.

Food is about place and *Farm Food* is about putting that place at the forefront of our culinary senses. A meal is not just about its ingredients but also about where the ingredients came from and the season, the time, and the people around the table.

A cuisine takes it cue from the climate, the occasion, and the cook. It reflects all of those things. It tells diners the intention and the desires and the goals of the meal. Are we sad or exalted, rich or poor, celebratory or simply hungry? We are telling a story with food. When I cook, sometimes I want to impress, get my guests to like me, or be consoled by those I invite to join me around this table.

I also want to eat great food. And not just any great food, but food grown here, made here, and about this beautiful place on Vashon Island. You might live down the street from my farm, across the country, or across the globe; it doesn't matter. I want folks to find the food that grows in their yards, that is for sale at their farmers' markets, and that reflects their life and surroundings. Food is about context and place and time. *Farm Food* is my way of bringing this experience to you.

— KURT
Vashon Island, Washington

Thirteen acres.

It is beautiful here. And special. Twenty-five years ago, with little thought, I left my tiny studio apartment in downtown Seattle behind for a life in the country, buying a ramshackle home on a scrubby piece of land on Vashon Island. I had little interest in being a farmer, at the time. Only after many years did I quit my job and work full time on what would, eventually, become Kurtwood Farms.

It has been fourteen years since I sold my Seattle restaurant and began growing food as my profession. I had been a cook and a restaurateur for many years, but I still came from the culture of buying all my food at the store. Little by little, I began living off of these thirteen acres, serving much-celebrated weekly dinners in the Cookhouse, each dish made entirely with fruits and vegetables, meats and cheeses, and herbs grown and foraged on or near the farm. The dinners have ended but living off the land certainly has not. If anything, more food is produced here than ever before.

Most of the farm is in pasture. It took most of the quarter century I have been here to clear the land. Few nice-looking trees were here when I arrived, but there were vast numbers of scrubby volunteer trees and shrubs: hawthorns with their violent thorns, Himalayan blackberries (the invasive scourge of this region), scotch broom, and stands of cherries that looked rather charming but were mostly just sturdy weeds.

These pastures feed my beautiful herd of Jersey cows. Growing up in the city, I never expected to spend my adult years with cows, but I welcome their addition to my life. They are gentle, except when they aren't. They make me smile. I appreciate their charms and coy nature until they cause me such grief that I want to immediately beef them and return to vegetable farming.

We milk them twice daily, every day of the year. Actually, Mario or Finn or Tim milks them twice daily. I, thankfully, rarely have to be in the milking parlor, cleaning the udders and teats of these dear ladies. For the first six years of the dairy, I was in the milking parlor every day, but now my schedule keeps me from performing this daily chore. On the rare occasions that all of my guys are away from the farm, I step in to round up the herd and line them up for their morning and evening milking. It is pleasurable if the weather is nice; dreadful if it is a blustery day with rain pelting down on the cow yards and large amounts of mud between me and the gates. The cows seem so much more personable when it is a lovely spring day; the same probably goes for me.

All that lovely Jersey milk heads to the milk room, where it is quickly cooled and then, depending on what is needed, poured into the pasteurizer vat for ice cream base or cheese. In the spring and summer, the great majority of the milk goes into ice cream; in cold days of autumn and the dead of winter, it is most likely all made into cheese.

Every week I spend time both at the farm and also at our Farm Shop in Seattle, where we sell ice cream and cheese. Living on the farm is an odd arrangement, a bit peculiar. Every day, I am in both my place of refuge and also my business. What is business and what is pleasure gets all mixed together. I look out my bedroom window in the Loghouse early in the morning and see Mario pulling up and flipping the lights on in the Cookhouse, occasionally blaring the music so loud that I can hear it. My laundry is done along with the bar towels and aprons from my farm shop and the multitude of towels used to clean the cows. Every morning, Tim or Finn sort the huge pile of clean laundry, folding up the bar towels and throwing my shorts or tee shirts or worn Carhartt jeans into a pile for me at the end of the long Douglas fir table in the Cookhouse. The farm's shower is just off of the kitchen and I tend to walk around while still dripping wet from the shower, looking for that shirt I like and know I washed early in the week, as an employee is sorting through cheese orders, washing chicken eggs, or weighing sugar for the ice cream base.

The centerpiece of the farm is the Cookhouse, a stand-alone building, a remarkable kitchen. The most handsome one I know. There is a wood-fired oven a few feet away north of the kitchen, and a large garden a short walk away to the south. There is never a shortage of ingredients to prepare a meal: fruits, vegetables, meats, and cheeses in abundance. A couple of cows are slaughtered every year, along with at least a couple of hogs. The butcher brings sides of beef and whole pigs into the kitchen to break them down and wrap up individual pieces of beautiful meat.

By the end of each month, a lot has happened on these thirteen acres. The kitchen never really seems to get cleaned and put away. There is always another project. Always something else to make, bottle, ferment, or brew. It feeds my restless soul. I always want to try something new. I always want to bake a different cake, scone, or pie, or find a new way to prepare the beef or pork. The cooler is filled with strange projects: some successful and some complete failures that end up going to the pigs.

I have often taken it all for granted. It isn't until I snap pictures or sit down to write that I realize I love it. Really love it. The weird and crazy part of it. The fact that I so rarely ever have a day when no one is here but me. The idea that I thrive on the activity until I want some solitude.

It is an unusual life, I would guess; served with great food, certainly. Quiet at night except for the spring frogs that never stop croaking during the early weeks of March. A hysterically short commute when I am at the farm for the whole day. Sometimes I think I miss the time when I milked the cows myself and made all the cheese myself and then tried to grow some plants in the garden, too. But then I remember how damn hard that was and how lucky I am to have people helping me here and at the farm shop. There were days of utter despair in the dark winter months when something would go wrong and I didn't have anyone to help me. On the dark, rainy days of winter, I can remember those days and find some joy in the simple parts of this farm.

OCTOBER

October.

One often thinks of July or perhaps August as the time of great abundance on the farm, as all of the tomatoes and basil and cucumbers at farmers markets would suggest. But the high summer months are just an overture to the great crescendo that is October. Each year, I am overwhelmed, and each year, I pledge to do better in preserving next year's harvest. This year was no different, with one exception.

The great trifecta of ways to utilize foods picked in this fall month includes freezing, canning, and of course, just eating fresh. This year I added a fourth: dehydrating. I went online and ordered a large multi-shelf dehydrator. Originally I only intended to use it to dry orange peels for an oranges 'n cream ice cream for the shop, but once I plugged it in on the kitchen counter, it became the go-to piece of equipment for weeks.

I remembered the back-to-the-land hippies of the 70s with their homemade dehydrators: a light bulb inside a wooden box with screens holding all manner of dried fruit and meat. I never really understood the fascination. Who wanted to eat dried fruit?

Then, once that gentle fan and warm heat filled the modern compartment, I understood. And then I was thrilled with the process.

There is an orchard here, not too large, just twenty trees: pears, apples, plums, quince, persimmons, Asian pears, and a few others as well. I planted them when I first established this farm, over two decades ago, and now they are all mature and producing vast amounts of fruit. Most land on the ground. Hard to believe that I could allow excellent fruit to fall, never to be eaten, but harvesting them is simply overwhelming.

For the past four weeks, I have been loading the shelves with fruit, trying out different methods and modes to produce tasty product. Some have been successful; others, less so. I'm still not entirely sure what will become of the rapidly filling shelves of dried fruits and vegetables.

Grapes — I have three decades-old grapevines and no idea what varieties they are. I rarely eat much of their rather abundant yield. This year, however, we pulled all of the grapes off their bunches and put them in the dehydrator. A couple of days later, we had a tidy amount of raisins. The method was simple: we pulled all of the fruit from the bunches and laid them out on the dehydrator's shelves. They rolled around at first but then, after a few hours, they began to dry and darken. A few held out for hours, bulking up into robust balloon shapes, before relenting to their transformation into raisins. Watching bright green and red grapes enter the dark box and come out a couple of days later as raisins—raisins!—was a wonderful experience. First Tim, then myself, and then friends who happened to have stopped by, looked at the final product and exclaimed, "They look just like raisins!" We now have a few jars full for winter baking, rum raisin ice cream, and mincemeat pie.

Pears — I originally tried, rather unsuccessfully, to dry pears with their peel intact. Sadly, I now have a couple pounds of dried-up pear-like leather. Not sure what will become of those. After some tinkering I discovered the best method was to peel the fruit, halve, and core it before drying it over medium heat over the course of a couple days. Tiny Seckel pears, although quite tasty and sweet while fresh, are much too small to bother with. We ate as many as possible during the couple of weeks when they were ripe and abundant.

Comice, when ripe, produced a tasty final product, but they tended to loose their shape while sticking to the mat. They also greatly resembled fried chicken parts: from tiny chickens, but still. Bosc pears work quite well, especially if they are just starting to ripen. When peeling the fruit, it should have just the hint of moisture starting on the surface. They hold their shape, concentrate a nice amount of sweetness, and have a good chewy texture that will store nicely through the dark months.

Chilies — The greenhouse always keeps a few pepper plants: sweet and spicy bells, and long, skinny cayenne. Although the bells respond best to roasting and pickling, the rest dry beautifully. Removing the core and seeds, and even slicing them lengthwise to open them up, helps the most. Once they are completely dry and brittle, a few seconds in a spice mill will produce the most fragrant, fresh chili powder. The powder needs to be placed in a sealed jar immediately afterward so they don't absorb the moist air and clump up. I smoked a handful of fresh chilies for a tremendous paprika. The excitement of seeing and smelling and tasting these

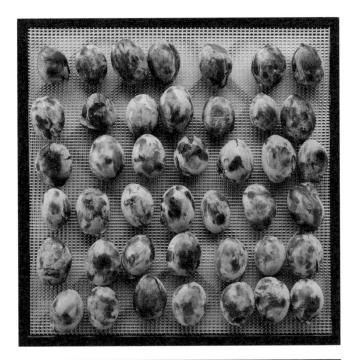

bright, deep red-colored powder is overwhelming. It is like pure alchemy—something so precious and beautiful coming from such simple chilies. Needless to say my winter cooking will be much spicier this year.

Persimmons — When the persimmons ripened later in the season, they too headed to the dehydrator. I tried a few methods, first slicing them crosswise into meaty slabs that felt like luscious, fresh tuna. They were bright orange and moist and glistening, and the outer peel kept them in tidy circles. I tended faithfully to them, flipping as needed to keep them from sticking to the web matting. And after a couple of days, they were dried orange discs, not terribly beautiful. I tasted them. They were most uninteresting.

Then I tried making hoshigaki-style persimmons, peeling slightly unripe persimmons and allow them to dry whole. After a few days of low heat in the dehydrator, they looked beautiful: shrunken and oblong with a dried stem still attached. The taste continued to be dull and uninteresting. I resorted to freezing the very ripe pulp of the remaining fresh fruits. All trying can't be a great success.

Tomatoes — 'Sun-dried' tomatoes have become so ubiquitous that I was hesitant to even try making some. Certainly there is no chance of sun drying tomatoes in this part of the country, with our not terribly hot summers and a large chance of possible precipitation. I had an abundance of fruit, so I sliced some in half and put them on the shelves of the miracle machine. Sliced was great; whole, not so much. Whole cherry tomatoes tended to plump up like balloons from the heat, yet dried nicely when sliced.

Oranges — There certainly aren't orange trees in the orchard, although we have grown them in pots over the years. During the dark winter months, however, I buy citrus as a welcome treat. The peels are removed with a peeler and then poached a couple of times in boiling water to remove the added wax; then they are boiled a third time in a simple syrup, drained, and dehydrated overnight until crisp. When the dried peels are pulverized in a spice grinder, they pack flavor into a vibrant orange dust. Added to ice cream, it is remarkable. Added to anything actually, it is remarkable.

Garlic — By October, I have long since harvested all of the garlic from the herb beds just outside the kitchen door. Yet late fall is the time to replant the best, plumpest cloves for next year's growing season. After I broke up the largest heads, the genetic stars went into the garden and the small, oddly shaped imperfect ones went into the dehydrator. I found slicing them worked best: they then dried quickly and crisply. Mistakenly, I tried pulverizing them in a spice mill like the orange peels and chilies. Although beautiful and fragrant at that moment, the dried cloves of garlic quickly clumped together and created not a useful garlic powder but just sticky lumps. Grinding to order is the way to go.

Plums — I have a few plum trees here but the most prolific is without question the Italian Prune Plum. You won't think a tree can produce such an abundance year after year until you have one of these varieties in your yard. Even so, I planted a second one right next to my original specimen a couple of years back. Not sure why; I guess I was just worried about not having enough. I now have enough, no question.

Dehydrating has opened a whole new world of Italian Prune Plums to me. Drying is the final state that these deep purple gems were designed for. Simply splitting the plums and removing the pit, then lining them up on the shelves of the dehydrator, is all that is needed. They slowly dry to chewy, sweet, dark glory. The only challenge is having enough room in one dehydrator to process all of the plums coming off of the tree. I may need a second machine next autumn. The labor takes hours but the results are worth it. They are sublime and have little similarity to the store-bought version we are familiar with. Prunes are my new best friends.

This part of the country is rich with apples. They are the main export on the eastern side of the state, where the climate and soil is ideally suited for apples. And yet, here on the other side of the mountains, where we have less heat in the summer and vastly more rain, apples still do quite well. I have planted a few trees over the years and also tried to keep the old trees that were here when I arrived productive, despite their age. I want to believe that those large, spreading trees, planted decades ago, are superior in flavor and shape and history. In practice, they are beyond their productive years. One by one I have removed them and replaced them with semi-dwarf varieties. The magic is gone, certainly, but the apples are delightful. When I have left this farm, many years from now, the next generation of homesteaders will marvel at my selections and covet the rambling old trees until they too give in and replace them.

Apples and their juice are the blood of this culture. We have no viable olives or citrus or grapes, but we do have a river of the sweet, golden drink that is apple juice. Most every garage and shed has a press of some sort stored away for its starring role each fall. Mine came from a widow who was gladly selling off her husband's possessions in the hopes of gaining some needed real estate in her garage. She knew little about the bulky wooden press except that I was excited to haul it away.

Generally I press what I have on the farm and work just hard enough to get a few gallons for the year. I could do better: I could pick every last fruit on my trees, save them, and even pick more from friends' orchards, but it feels like work at that point and at a busy time of year. This year, I did what I tend to avoid—the group pressing. One of my employees, Elizabeth, had seen the press near the kitchen and inquired. She had a prolific King apple tree and hoped to press them at the farm. I acquiesced and soon we had her family and a couple of my guys out making cider.

It is such a cliché at this point: the weekend cider party. New folks move to the island, buy a shiny new press, and have friends from the city over together for warm cinnamon doughnuts and hot, spiced cider. It is right up there with giving their property a cute farm name. I can make fun of it: I did the same a couple decades ago. Now I watch as new neighbors discover that there is sweet juice inside those shiny apples and that they can release it, something they never did when they lived in the city. It is as if they just discovered this great feat of fruit alchemy.

Elizabeth brought her family and most importantly, brownies, so I was all in. She also brought many bushels of sweet and juicy Kings. We got a quick line of activities together and in a couple of hours' time, we had all of the containers filled. The apples were washed and chopped as they fell into the basket and then pressed, the juice flowing out and down the wooden container into waiting buckets. It is an old and never changed system. There is nothing digital to it. Nothing modern or electric or new. Just an old beechwood press and steel screw that brings the wooden platen down onto the chopped apples. I have done this many times and hope to continue for many more years. We always need apple juice to get us through the coming winter.

The dried, pressed, and crumbly apples, also called the spent mash, get sent to the pigs just a few feet away in their sty. They relish this treat. Every few minutes, another bucketful arrives and they attempt to keep up. I want to think that when we slaughter these pigs in a few weeks' time, the pork will be apple-scented, but mostly I just think it is a divine day for these happy pigs. By the next dawn, they will have found every last bit of sweet morsel and will be waiting for their regular ration. All that remains from this weekend will be the containers of juice and a few smiling hogs.

The juice has a few different uses. These are my favorites and the ones I look forward to each year.

The first use is simply as a fresh, sweet juice. It's best the same day, right out of the press, completely connected to the source. Apples are dropped into the upper hopper and a refreshing beverage is in my glass a couple of minutes later. We drink a lot this way. I like when it has just a bit of tannin, a hint of edge and depth and adultness; not like the simple juice from the store. Not like a juice box at all.

As we are grown-ups, we made cocktails with it that night. Actually, for a few nights after. They were that good.

Apple Cider Cocktail

fresh apple juice, *4 ounces (120 ml)*
Kentucky bourbon, *2 ounces (60 ml)*
Rachel's ginger beer (or similar local ginger beer)
lemon, *cut into wedges*

In a large, glass cocktail tumbler combine juice and bourbon, add ice cubes halfway and then top off the glass with Rachel's ginger beer and a squeeze of lemon juice.

YIELD: *Cocktails for two.*

Another good use is making apple cider vinegar. I'll fill two five-gallon car-boys with fresh cider, then pitch a small amount of hard cider yeast into a cup of gently warmed juice and let it proof for a few minutes until the yeast is activated by the heat and sweetness of the fresh apple juice. When it's bubbly and alive, I add it to the full carboys and let it go to work. The yeast will eat the sugars in the sweet cider and create alcohol. It is simple process but one with profound results. Gone is the sweetness of the cider and in its place is the excitement of the alcohol.

On the top of each carboy are small airlocks to let the gas created by the process out without allowing outside air in. I let them bubble and gurgle for a few weeks until the busyness of fall has given way to the quiet of winter. Some of the cider could certainly be drunk as is, fortified with alcohol to become a much more serious beverage. But I want it all for vinegar. I will pour the contents of these two carboys into a large French oak barrel that, by this time of year, is only half full with a vinegar mother and the rest of last year's batch. The mother will consumer the alcohol in the hard cider and transform it to vinegar. It is a tremendous process from apples to sweet apple juice to hard cider and then to apple cider vinegar, which has deep flavor and complexities and acid without being harsh. I have no recipe for apple cider vinegar, but the method is so very simple. You'll need an existing mother. I bought mine years ago at a beer supply store but I am sure they are available online. Vinegar needs warmth and a bit of air to develop. And time. It's not an instant process. I keep a large oak keg on the floor of the Cookhouse and I initially added the vinegar mother to the keg when it was partially filled with hard apple cider. Over time, the alcohol is converted to acid and the vinegar remains. Now, each fall, I top off the keg with new hard cider and give it a few weeks to activate and fully acidify.

Once the cider is fermenting and I've had a few of the fresh cocktails, I begin to cook with the juice. A ruby-colored cider reduction is well worth the effort to produce. It is silky and sticky and sweet and depth of flavor is remarkable.

Apple Cider Redux

This is one of my favorite recipes. In fact, it is barely a recipe and more of a technique. There are no measurements, just a simple process, and yet I have never failed to be impressed with the result.

Take a large volume of fresh apple juice. Go to the farmers' market in the autumn and buy a gallon (or two or three). Pour it all into a large stock pot and turn on the heat. Bring it to a full boil and then lower it to a good simmer. We want to reduce its volume by boiling off the excess water. It will take a while; the amount of time will vary depending on the volume. Just watch it reduce by seventy-five percent and then begin to test it. Take a spoonful, place it on a saucer, and let it cool. If it is a deep mahogany color and has a bit of sugary syrupiness to it, it's ready. If it is just hot apple juice, keep simmering until it looks rich, thick, and sweet, with a huge apple flavor.

This apple cider reduction also translates beautifully into an apple gastrique. It is a terrible word, redolent of a horrible stomach ailment, but the alternative—sweet and sour sauce—is more indicative of bad Chinese food. Simply adding vinegar, preferably apple cider vinegar, adds the acidity necessary to balance out the sweetness of the reduction. Think of it as balsamic vinegar, but based on apples instead of grapes, and use it in the same ways: for salads or for drizzling on strawberries and peaches.

The basic starting point I use is 3 tablespoons (45 ml) of apple cider vinegar to 1 cup (240 ml) of apple cider redux. That will give you a sweet and also acidic sauce.

Pancakes with Redux

This is a simple recipe I should be able to remember, but I never do and so I always text my buddy Matt for it. He knows it by heart: he has kids and loves to cook some up for them, and himself, often. I think of him when I make pancakes. It's his thing. It's what I think of when I imagine him with his kids. He's that dad. The good dad. The guy that makes pancakes every Saturday. Probably every Sunday as well. And most likely without chocolate chips, an obvious cheap shot at getting your kids to like you. He doesn't need to resort to chocolate chips; his kids already love him. This is the recipe he texts me:

MATT'S FAMILY PANCAKES

milk, *2 cups (240 ml)*
eggs, *2*
flour, *2 cups (240 g)*
baking powder, *2 tablespoons (30 g)*
butter, melted, *2 tablespoons (30 ml)*
sugar, *2 tablespoons (30 g)*
vinegar, *1 teaspoon (5 ml)*
salt, *pinch*
baking soda, *pinch*

Melt the butter and set aside. In a large mixing bowl, sift the dry ingredients together. Whisk eggs quickly with the milk. Combine milk and egg mixture with dry ingredients and mix gently but thoroughly. Add melted butter.

Ladle batter onto medium skillet with a bit of fat. When the bubbles burst, flip. Cook until both sides are nicely browned.

Please don't use non-stick pans. For years, I used those at my restaurant for frying eggs and making omelets. And every few weeks, I would need to replace them because the non-stick surface was gone. Oh, certainly some of that was removed in the dishwasher, but I just don't like the idea of including tiny fragments of the coating in your pancakes or eggs.

YIELD: *8 medium pancakes.*

Once the fresh fruit was dried and stored away in the larder in jars, I needed a use for it. Certainly I could spend the winter months nibbling on the pears and prunes and raisins, but I was excited to use them to create something special from the dried bits of summer. Preserving them in alcohol was the most successful and the most enjoyable method.

Master Recipe for Dried Fruit in Alcohol

dried fruit, *1 pound (.45 kg)*
spirits, *2 cups (475 ml)*
organic cane sugar, *1 cup (200 g)*
spirits, *2 tablespoons (30 ml) or more — optional*

Place the fruit, sugar, and two cups of spirits in a wide saucepan over a low flame and slowly bring the mixture to a simmer. Once the alcohol is hot, it has a tendency to ignite on a gas burner, so be prepared. The blue flames dancing across the pot can be a beautiful sight, but if you want to put it out, just cover the pot with a lid. Keeping the heat low will also help avoid a fire. Allow the mixture to simmer for at least twenty minutes or until the alcohol and sugar have turned into a deep, dark syrup and the fruits are opened and ready. Add the withheld tablespoons of spirits to the cooled fruit in syrup and mix well. Allow to cool completely before placing in jars.

Prunes in Armagnac — The classic, and one of the very best. Serve the boozy dried plums alone at the end of the meal, or even better, on vanilla ice cream. This is sure to get you through the dark winter nights.

Comice pears in Poire William — The luscious Comice pears that dried into shapes resembling small, fried chicken thighs make much more sense when plumped up in pear brandy. They are full of flavor, sticky, and orange and remind me so much of the heat at the end of the summer, when these fruits were ripe and plentiful. When I am nibbling on these little nuggets of summer, I am immediately taken back to the days when I walked through the orchard and my toes would get covered in rotting windfall pears, my Birkenstocks becoming a mucky mess.

Raisins in Dark Rum — I thought the dried grapes out of the dehydrator were exceptional. At the time, I showed them off to anyone who came by the kitchen, but now I have found they become even more delicious when cooked in dark rum.

I now have a row of these dried fruits canned in syrupy alcohol and lined up on the shelf here in the Cookhouse. I add them to this or that. Or just drizzle them over ice cream. Like I need another reason to eat ice cream.

———————————

I have made this cake every year for many years; it was a regular offering at my restaurant Cafe Septieme in Seattle. With standard prunes, it is quite good. With prunes grown here and cooked with Armagnac, it is extraordinary. This is a large recipe and will make two cakes. They are exceptional when fresh out of the oven; a bit messy to cut with the prunes and all, but light and fragrant. Save the second cake for a couple of days. When it is fully cool and settled down, it will slice brilliantly and have a lovely density and texture. So make two: you will need them both.

Prune Bundt Cake

butter, *2 cups (500 g)*
organic cane sugar, *2 cups (400 g)*
eggs, *8*
egg yolks, *2*
all-purpose flour, *4 ½ cups (540 g)*
baking powder, *2 teaspoons (10 g)*
prunes in Armagnac, *2 cups with liquid (475 ml)*

Preheat oven to 375°F (190°C).

Butter and gently flour a large Bundt cake mold, or two medium-sized 8" (20 cm) molds, and set aside.

Cream butter and sugar in mixer until fully combined and lightened. Slowly add eggs and then yolks one by one until they are well incorporated. Sift together dry ingredients and quickly incorporate in mixer. Remove batter from mixer and fold in prunes and liquid with rubber spatula. Fill Bundt pan or pans.

Bake for 60 – 75 minutes until knife in center comes out cleanly. Cake will rise, crack open, and brown nicely on the edges. Let cool for ten minutes or until cake begins to separate from the sides. Invert gently onto cooling rack. Allow to fully cool. Slice and serve with whipped cream with a bit of Armagnac syrup added to the cream before whisking.

YIELD: *2 cakes, each enough to satisfy eight people.*

I love these prunes. I want to use them for my favorite recipes. They worked very well in ricotta fritters. When I tried these the first time, I was thinking of Bavarian knudel, the dumplings filled with plums.

Look for a ricotta with no stabilizers or gums listed in the ingredients. The measurements will be greatly different than these. And although they are delightful as soon as they are out of the oil and still warm, reheating them later in the oven works tremendously well.

Ricotta Fritters with Prunes

flour, *¾ cup (90 g)*
baking powder, *2 teaspoons (10 g)*
ricotta, *1 cup (220 g)*
egg yolks, *2*
sugar, *2 tablespoons (30 g)*
fat for deep frying, *2 quarts (2 liters)*
powdered sugar
prunes in Armagnac

Sift flour and baking powder together in bowl. Add ricotta, yolks, and sugar to dry mixture and blend well. Form into balls with a teaspoon, pushing a quarter prune into each ball. Heat oil in a deep pot on stovetop until it reaches 350°F (175°C), then drop ricotta balls into hot oil. They will drop and then rise to the surface. When they have browned, use a strainer to pull them out and place them on paper towels to cool. Dredge them in powdered sugar before serving.

YIELD: *16 balls, each approximately 1 inch (25 mm) in diameter.*

PLEASE NOTE: If oil is too hot, ricotta balls will brown before the center is cooked. If it's too cold, it will overcook before browning.

Persimmons are still plentiful this month and ripening into November, depending on the weather. I tried drying the first harvest of the year in early October while the rest ripened fully on the tree until they were sweet and nearly liquid. And, just as I was realizing I didn't know what to do with these very ripe ones, I found a use: persimmon vinegar. Thumbing through a book on preserves, I found a recipe for this tasty thing. And the directions fit my personality: let them rot until they turn into vinegar, then strain them. I could do that.

I took as many very ripe, but not ruined, persimmons—hachiya—as I could find and removed the stems and seeds but kept the skins. Then I placed them all in a ceramic container and covered it with a fine cheesecloth before leaving it out in the kitchen. The fruit flies tried but never succeeded to get into the sweetly rotting pot. After a few weeks, it became more and more liquid, and then fermented as the sweet sugars of the fruit changed into alcohol. After a few more weeks and a bit of luck, the alcohol will turn to vinegar. In the springtime, I hope to drain the remaining solids and have a deep orange, sour liquid. It is an interesting culinary technique: benign neglect that will hopefully result in a profound ingredient. As I look at it now, near the end of autumn, I am optimistic but cautious.

NOVEMBER

November.

A cow—Dinah 2.0—smacked me in the eye a few years back. I was milking the young heifer and her tail flew, the errant tip hitting me spot on. I thought nothing of it until three days later when my retina tore, filling my eye will blood. Three unsuccessful surgeries later, I was left with a good story but no sight out of one eye.

I easily learned to live with this singular vision. It really is rather simple. The only downside is a lack of depth of field in very close encounters: routinely, a cashier will hand me change and I will miss it by an inch or two, quarters falling to the ground. A tiny inconvenience and thankfully it wasn't obvious to anyone looking at me.

And then last week, my good eye began to fail. The retina there began to tear and detach. I knew the signs and went in to have it checked. The doctor tried to quickly reattach it in the office but when that failed to hold, I was quickly scheduled for more surgery.

It was a beautiful November morning when I woke at the farm, my surgery scheduled for early in the afternoon. Cold but not icy out, with a thick layer of mist settling over the pastures. The sun was just beginning to break above the trees to light the fields when I finished my coffee.

I grabbed my camera and a wide lens and walked up from the Cookhouse to the upper pastures where Mario had left hay for the cows. They had just arrived and begun eating when I pulled off the lens cap and began to shoot.

I took on this renewed love of shooting pictures just a year and a few weeks earlier, yet this is what I feared the most that morning: losing the ability to capture beautiful images. I knew what failed eye surgeries were like—I had had three already. I knew that it was possible that this was my last day with eyesight. And this is what I wanted to do before getting on the ferry to Seattle and heading to the hospital: take pictures of my cows and farm. I was in tears, sadder than I think I have ever been. And also alone, just me and a dozen or so cows gently chewing on hay for company. They were unaware of my thoughts as I walked around them, slowing taking a roll of film on my favorite Hasselblad. I didn't want to be too dramatic, too worried, too scared—but I was. The surgeon and my friends has been very optimistic, but it was my sight that was on the line and I wanted to remember this morning even if there was the chance I would never see these images. Someone might. And with luck it would be me.

Nature cooperated. The light was gorgeous and special. The mist hung around the cows and started falling down the side of the hill. As the sun gently rose, it hit first the upper trees, then the lower trees, and then the pastures, burning off that mist with its heat. In thirty minutes' time, I was out of film and the fields were bathed in the bright morning sun of winter. And then I slowly walked down the hill, trying to hold onto this moment.

The film sat on my desk for three weeks until I came back to the farm after staying with friends as I recuperated. My sight returned and I developed that roll. To my great joy, the images were beautiful and saved that moment for me: the day that I was unsure of my future. The morning that I appreciated all that I had even if there was the possibility of losing it. I still tear up as I look at these photos.

A few days later, it was Thanksgiving and I had more than ever to be thankful for. Both for my vision but also for the friends around me who cared for my blind self during those first few days when I couldn't feed myself or care for myself or even walk without hitting walls and doors and furniture. They put the fork in my hand and helped me eat. They calmed me down when I panicked over the possibility of living in the total darkness. Not sure that it was the easiest way to appreciate friends, but it was the way that got through to me.

Food was a way to thank them and appreciate them. We slaughtered the last two pigs of the year at the farm that week. Winter was quickly arriving and mud appeared in what had been a perfect sty only days before. I wanted to be the guy who could just thank his friends for their friendship and love, but I still needed to do some accounting. Some payment in kind. I dropped off a few pork roasts and pork bellies and shanks. They loved it and I felt a bit better, too.

Thanksgiving had a few things I really loved. The mincemeat pie was outstanding. And the pickles. Pickles are such simple things, but rather important to start a meal. You can't just jump in and start chomping on a turkey leg. It needs to be a slow dance. Pickles do that, and these, made from cucumbers, peppers, and shallots, did very well.

And then some riced potatoes, cooked with milk and butter and salt. I was thinking of mashing them, but that seemed crude for a holiday meal. Ricing is an elegant approach for such a simple tuber.

Master Pickle Recipe

apple cider vinegar or rice wine vinegar, *2 cups (475 ml)*
water, *½ cup (120 ml)*
sugar, *1 tablespoon (15 g)*
kosher salt, *2 tablespoons (30 g)*
black peppercorns, *1 tablespoon (15 mg)*

Combine all ingredients in a two-quart sauce pan and bring to a boil. Pour hot vinegar over the vegetables in a heat-proof jar. Make sure all vegetables are covered with vinegar mixture and allow them to cool fully. Cover and refrigerate. The pickles will be ready in a couple of days. Although apple cider vinegar is plentiful here and we use it for pickles, rice wine vinegar also produces a fine pickle.

Pickled Lemon Cucumbers — Trim off the ends and thinly slice. These cucumbers are very tender, so allow the vinegar mixture to cool fully before pouring it over the cucumbers.

Pickled Whole Shallots — Peel off the dried outer layer from the shallots and trim nicely. Add shallots to sauce pan and return vinegar mixture to a boil, then turn off the heat. Let rest for a few minutes before moving shallots to a container for storage.

Roasted Red Peppers — Roast the whole peppers directly on the gas flames of the stove until fully blackened, then set aside. When cool enough to handle, rub the char off. Once the peppers are fully cleaned, cut off the stem and slice the peppers lengthwise into wide strips. Pack the sliced roasted peppers in glass jars. Let the vinegar mixture cool and then pour over roasted pepper slices.

Pickled Pumpkin — De-seed and trim the hard rind off the pumpkin, then slice thinly on a mandolin. Pour boiling hot vinegar mixture over the sliced pumpkin and allow to cool.

Mincemeat Pie

venison, ½ *pound (230 g)*
beef suet, ½ *pound (230 g)*
brown sugar, 12 *ounces (270 g)*
molasses, ¾ *cup (180 ml)*
apple cider, 2 *cups (475 ml)*
dried pears, 2 *cups (300 g)*
raisins, 1 ½ *cup (225 g)*
apples, peeled, cored, and diced, 2
quince, peeled, cored, and diced, 1
Calvados, ¾ *cup (180 ml)*
salt, *to taste*

Combine dried pears and raisins with apple cider in a large bowl and allow to plump for ten minutes. Combine remaining ingredients in a large, heavy saucepan and begin to cook over medium high heat. Stir as needed to keep from sticking. Add dried fruit and apple cider mixture to the sauce pan and continue cooking. Lower heat as it begins to thickens. Mincemeat will begin to darken and become viscous and bubbly (30 – 45 minutes). Allow to fully cool. Prepare tart shells.

Although I baked pastries for my restaurant for many years, I rarely created my own baking formulas. I have no illusions about my skill with baking formulas; I rely on the masters of the craft. I look to Nick Malgieri for the best recipes for pastry. His book, *Perfect Pastry,* has been on my shelf for years and is my go-to.

SUGAR CRUST AFTER NICK MALGIERI

all-purpose flour, *2 cups (240 g)*
organic cane sugar, *½ cup (100 g)*
salt, *¼ teaspoon (1.25 g)*
baking powder, *½ teaspoon (2.5 g)*
butter, *¼ pound (120 g)*
large eggs, 2

Sift together flour, sugar, salt, and baking soda in a medium bowl. Cut butter into small slices and rub butter into flour with your fingertips, gently smearing it until all the butter is incorporated. The mixture will be crumbly.

With a fork, rapidly stir eggs in a small bowl. Add eggs into the flour/butter mixture and with your hands combine all gently and quickly, pulling the parts together. Form a ball and divide it into two pieces. Create two discs of flattened dough. Wrap individually and cool and rest for at least thirty minutes.

Unwrap each individual disk, roll out to a circle larger than the tart pan. Lay the dough into the pan, pressing well into the corners. Trim off any excess on the top and chill fully. Finish second tart shell as well. When both are chilled and rested, fill with foil and dried beans and bake blind at 350°F (175°C) until bottom of tart is gently cooked but not fully cooked. Remove foil and beans and allow to cool.

Divide fully chilled mincemeat into two portions and spoon into tart shells. Mincemeat will need to be spread out with a spatula evenly. Bake in the middle of the oven until the tart shells are fully cooked. Remove from oven, allow to cool and remove tart rings.

YIELD: *Makes two 9" (22.5 cm) pies.*

I doubt that this mincemeat pie needs anything else, but it is still nice to serve it with some ice cream. For me, caramel is the ideal winter flavor: deep, rich, and intense with dark, sugar flavors. It is also another menu item for Thanksgiving dinner that can be prepared days in advance.

Caramel Ice Cream

organic cane sugar, *2 ½ cups (500 g)*
egg yolks, *6*
tapioca starch, *4 tablespoons (60 g)*
salt, *pinch*
milk, *3 cups (700 ml)*
cream, *3 cups (700 ml)*

Whisk together ½ cup (100 g) sugar, yolks, tapioca starch, sugar and salt. Set aside.

In heavy, small saucepan, caramelize 2 cups sugar. Add 2 cups sugar to a small, heavy saucepan and turn the heat to medium. With a wooden spoon, stir the sugar as it begins to brown and melt, breaking up any clumps as they form. Over the course of a few minutes, the sugar will completely transform into a thick, golden liquid. Continue until the sugar is dark, steaming, and smells like caramel. Take great care not to touch the caramel. Immediately but slowly pour in 2 cups of milk. The cooked sugar will splatter and pop when the milk is added. Continue to heat at a slow simmer until caramel is fully melted into milk.

When caramel is fully incorporated, slowly pour it into the egg and sugar mixture, whisking constantly. Combine the caramel with remaining milk and cream in a large sauce pan.

Slowly cook until sauce has thickened and fully combined. Pour through sieve into mixing bowl, cover, and chill overnight.

Freeze according to churn instructions.

YIELD: *Makes 2 quarts (2 liters).*

I love the traditional Thanksgiving menu, but it needs some help. I just can't eat the cranberry sauce that we grew up with any longer. I actually don't enjoy cranberries, really. And so, this year, we had tomato chutney. It is savory, sweet, and nuanced, and works very well with turkey and riced potatoes.

Tomato Chutney

tomatoes, peeled and cored, *5 pounds (2.25 kg)*
onions, peeled, cored, and chopped, *1 pound (450 g)*
dried pears, *½ pound (250 g)*
raisins, *½ pound (250 g)*
organic cane sugar, *1 ¾ pound (800 g)*
apple cider vinegar, *32 fluid ounces (1 liter)*

Clean and prepare all the fruits and vegetables. Place in a large saucepan together with the rest of the ingredients. Bring to a boil, stirring often. Reduce to a slow simmer and cook, still stirring often.

After an hour and a half, the mixture will start to stick and the color will deepen and become glossy. Let it continue to cook, making sure it doesn't burn, until the mixture is viscous and thick. Spoon into jars, seal, and allow the chutney to settle for a few days. Make extra for gifts and to keep in the cooler for yourself. Vary the ingredients wildly. I always have a bounty of pears and grapes, so I use them, but it's a versatile recipe. Just be sure to make it before you run out of tomatoes in the garden. I tend to use the very last ones of the season.

I haven't included a detailed recipe for roast turkey here. You can find those instructions in many places. But I can just say that my holiday life changed when I switched to spatchcocking the turkey. For those unused to this peculiar term, it means flattening the unwieldy bird. I flip it onto its breasts and completely cut out the backbone and neck. Then I gently open up the turkey, cracking the breastbone in the process. A bit of scoring with a knife helps speed the process. After the bird has been spatchcocked, I dry it, salt it heavily on the inside, then flip it over and salt

the skin before placing it on a large sheet pan. It will fit on one shelf of my admirably large oven but leave lots of room on the other shelf for warming side dishes.

I tend to cook the turkey fairly early in the day, allowing it to cool and then bringing it back to temperature just before we eat. My guests are never on time. Never. And I need to care less. I need to enjoy my fiends. I like my friends and the years when I have stood there in the kitchen, indignant at their tardiness, and then they feel they should drink and talk with the rest of the group... I like to have it ready when they are ready. I'm not here to control them. Now I know when the turkey is just about cooked. I can bring it back to temperature with a few minutes. No one can time when to remove a thirty-pound roasted bird based on when you think you will need it. It's a holiday, a day to be thankful, not a job to be accomplished. And I love the opportunity to cook for friends and enjoy this day. The spatchcocked turkey is my new best friend.

DECEMBER

December.

This is, first and foremost, a dairy farm. We raise Jersey cows, milk them, and produce cheese or ice cream from their milk. There is a singular concept in dairy farms that is often overlooked: cows produce milk to provide for their calves. They do not produce it at will but rather at the time of their calving, or freshening, as we dairymen call it. And so, in order to have a supply of milk, we have many calves born here at the farm. If we kept all of the calves or all of the mothers, our herd would grow larger and larger every year. My land is finite so we need to keep the size of the herd constant. Although we sell off the bull calves quickly, we tend to keep most of the female—heifer—calves on the farm. The only way we can keep the herd size constant is by slaughtering the oldest milking cows.

I have little problem with this. They produce high quality beef that feeds the farm's employees. Their meat gives me something else to sell here, keeping the farm profitable. And it keeps the cows that are producing milk in great health so their milk is of high quality. There are times when I do get attached to a particular cow, but I have accepted this as the model that runs this enterprise.

And so, this month, we slaughtered the oldest cow in the herd. The butcher was scheduled the first week in December and thankfully it was dry and relatively mild weather when he arrived. He is experienced and calm and talented at his chosen profession. I often wonder how he has done this job for decades. He first slaughtered sheep for me over twenty years ago and he is still on the job. I hire him for the cows primarily because they are large, heavy animals and I don't have the equipment or the interest in slaughtering them myself.

I used to keep cows here for much too long, letting them live until invariably the vet would be called to solve this or that or a cow would die unexpectedly in the field and we had to quickly bury its body far beneath the pasture. That was

worse. That was wasteful. Now we slaughter cows before they have any problems and share the meat with friends and employees. Actually, I share the meat with employees and sell it to friends, but that's just a detail.

I think these cows have great lives. They are well fed. It's calm and low stress here. And then there is one bad day; with luck, just a bad couple of seconds. I hope my life has just one bad day. A single shot takes them down instantly. And then they change from cows to beef, and feed all of us here.

Lauren comes out to the farm after the beef from the butchered cow has hung for ten days. She's the butcher that we hire to break down the sides into small roasts and steaks and grind. She's a badass and good at her job. It is a physical job, really a craft, and an important one. I want there to always be tough butchers to call on this island of mine.

It takes a few hours for Lauren and a couple of assistants to finish their work. The tables in the Cookhouse are spread with beef and bones and knives and grinders. Walking through the kitchen, it is very clear that this is no longer a cow. It is meat, good meat.

When Lauren has finished, there is a row of boxes filled with white paper-wrapped packages. Some will go into my freezer after the rest is distributed, but a packet or two will be fresh in my cooler. She has saved me a small bit of steak for my dinner.

No one is around tonight so I make beef tartar, just for me. The meat is certainly fresh, just cooled.

Beef Tartar

lean, fresh beef, preferably from the leg, *4 ounces (180 g)*
egg yolk, fresh pastured and separated from white, *1*
stone-ground mustard, *1 tablespoon (15 ml)*
pickles, *to taste*
rye bread, *1 loaf*

Trim any sinew or fat or silver skin from the beef and discard, saving only the best meat. With a Chinese cleaver slice the beef into thin tranches and then slice those again lengthwise. Continue into a small dice and then finely chop with the cleaver.

Make a small mound and add the yolk.

Toast a half dozen small squares of rye bread and serve with mustard and pickles.

YIELD: *Makes enough for two as a starter or one as a meal.*

This is one of the dishes that I like to eat in situ, on the chopping block in the kitchen where it is made. I like the connection it makes between the beef and the meal. Transferring the tartare to a beautiful plate and taking it into the dining room feels forced and inauthentic. Standing at the long butcher block table where the chopped beef and toast and egg yolk and mustard are all laid out, I can pop a dark beer and drink it from the bottle while making myself a delightful meal. Hours ago, Lauren brought in two sides of beef and now, as the day comes to a close, I can toast to the cow that gave me and my friends nourishment for the coming months.

———————————

There are few dishes that embody this season and this place as much as a Bolognese sauce with noodles. It just tastes like here. It's dark, rich, and fatty. And a bit elegant and tasty, too. Most of the ingredients are from here: the vegetables and the cider and the meats. The eggs from my chickens make golden noodles. Even if you don't have a farm, you can still make this dish yourself. It will be great.

Bolognese Sauce

ground beef, *1 pound (450 g)*
ground pork, *½ pound (225 g)*
large carrots, peeled and finely sliced, *2*
shallots, peeled and finely diced, *3*
garlic clove, peeled and finely diced, *1*
butter, *2 tablespoons (30 g)*
tomato sauce, *1 quart (950 ml)*
hard cider, *12 ounces (350 ml)*
bay, oregano, thyme and parsley, *a small handful in total, tied with string into bouquet garni*

In heavy-bottomed sauce pan, cook pork and beef together, using their own fat, until fat has fully rendered and the meats are cooked through (between 5 – 10 minutes).

Add diced carrots, shallots, and garlic together with butter. On medium heat, stir together with beef and pork until everything is incorporated and butter has melted. Cook until vegetables sweat and begin to cook through (another 5 – 10 minutes).

Add 12 ounces of hard cider and bouquet garni to pot.

Bring to a simmer, then lower heat and allow ingredients to reduce slightly before adding tomato sauce and bringing back to a simmer on medium heat.

Cook slowly for 45 minutes until beef is tender and has lost its firmness. Remove bouquet garni and season with salt and pepper. Serve over noodles.

YIELD: *Ample for four to six hungry folks.*

Master Pasta Recipe

all-purpose flour, *1 cup (120 g)*
eggs, *2*

Mound the flour on the counter, then make a well large enough to hold two eggs in the center of the flour. Crack the eggs into the center of the flour. Mix the eggs with a fork until the yolks and whites are combined and then begin adding flour with the fork. Slowly add more and more flour until the flour is fully combined with the eggs. Bring the combined egg and flour mixture together into a ball.

With your hands, knead dough until smooth, then wrap in plastic wrap and set aside to hydrate (about 30 minutes).

Unwrap dough and divide into smaller pieces. Roll out individually in pasta machine, laminating as needed, until dough is very thin and smooth. Set full length of dough aside on counter to dry. Continue on with the remaining dough. When sheets are firm and nearly dry but still bendable, cut them into 12" lengths, discarding ends. Gently and loosely roll up each individual sheet and cut to desired width. Unroll and allow to dry fully. On a hot, dry day the sheets of pasta will dry in just a couple of minutes, on a wet winter day it could take at least a half hour.

Cook the noodles in salted boiling water till done, drain. Toss with Bolognese sauce and serve.

As soon as Lauren has finished breaking down the cow, there are so many tidy packages of beef that it looks like a butcher's Christmas has arrived. Each packet has the name of the cut written on the side, along with the date. I will divide them up: some for my employees, some for myself, and some for friends. What remains in the kitchen are two large hotel pans filled with bones. She has scraped them well and cut each bone in half, but it still takes up a lot of space. The first thing I will do is dig through them and find the femurs—the long, straight leg bones. Those, I will set aside to cook the marrow and make compound butter with. The remaining bones are used for stock. The stainless steel hotel pans full of bones are placed in the oven at a high heat to roast. I have a friend, an excellent chef, who swears that it is better to not roast them. Roasting causing the stock to get bitter. He uses tomatoes to darken his stock. He is probably correct; he is a much better cook than I will ever be. Still, I like my method. I like the smell in the kitchen. I like the deep mahogany color of the meat that remains on the knuckles, ribs, and legs of my cow. It is also how I have always done it. You can try his method. It's probably great, but I love this one.

Halfway through the roasting, I cut up some onions and add them to the pile of bones in the oven. After three hours, I remove the two hotel pans and shift the contents into two large stockpots, then fill them with cold water and add all the vegetables I had on hand. And then I turn on the heat and bring them to a slow simmer. If I can get the gas just right, I will leave it on all night. There is little or no possibility of the pots boiling dry; mostly they are just very warm through the dark evening. Then, in the morning, I can open the doors and smell delicious beef stock simmering on the range.

Once the stock cools a bit, it can be drained into a smaller stockpot and allowed to sit undisturbed for the rest of the day. The fat will rise to the top and clump. Unless I can get the stockpot to fit into the refrigerator, it won't become a hard layer, but it is still rigid enough to lift out with a wide spoon spatula. Then I can begin to boil the stock down, rapidly, steam rising with force from the two stockpots on the stove. They boil and boil and boil until the stock is halfway done.

Freezing bags full of rich bone broth has tremendous value. It's simple to reach into the freezer to make soup or to braise some beef later in the winter. But I much more enjoy making beef demi-glaze. I reserve a portion of the beef stock and then move it to a smaller stockpot and reduce it even further, till it is viscous and deep brown. The final liquid might condense down to a quart after an initial amount of two gallons. It will contain a large amount of gelatin and, when cool, will be extremely solid. I keep it in a mason jar in the refrigerator and carve out spoonfuls to add to this or that project, giving it an additional jolt of beefy richness and body.

Beef Marrow Compound Butter

beef femur bones, *6 pounds (2.75 kg)*
room temperature butter, *1 cup (240 g)*
lemon thyme

Roast bones in a Pyrex container for 45 minutes in a hot oven. Let them cool until you can handle them easily, but don't let them cool too much. Dig the marrow out of the bones with a thin knife or a chopstick. Place the marrow in a small mixing bowl. Add the drippings and crunchies from the Pyrex dish. While still warm, add butter and mix well with a wooden spoon until fully incorporated. Add the lemon thyme leaves and fully combine with butter.

Take two large pieces of plastic wrap, at least a foot long on each side, and lay them flat on the counter. Divide the compound butter into two small log shapes and set one on each piece of plastic wrap, a couple of inches from the bottom. Roll the plastic wrap lengthwise around one of the logs, continuing until the plastic wrap is completely wrapped around the it, leaving plastic "handles" on each side. With one hand on each handle, roll the wrapped butter back and forth across the counter until the interior feels tight and the shape is smooth. Once this is process is complete, the ends of the plastic wrap can be folded over and the wrapped butter can be cooled in the refrigerator. Allow it to sit overnight.

To use, set it out at least half an hour before use so the butter has time to temper. When it is at that perfect spot, softened but not soft, slice ¼" (6 mm) off. Placed on a hot steak just off the grill, it will gently melt down into the cracks in the thick beefsteak. Once summer arrives and green beans are ripe in the garden, I intend to set out a platter of the steaming beans and add slices of this luscious compound butter. But in wintertime, a grilled steak is my best option.

YIELD: *Approximately 1 cup (250 g).*

Remarkably, I do manage to eat a vegetable or two during the winter. This soup is ideal for December. The carrots, onions, and potatoes I harvested in the fall are still in great shape, but their quality is starting to diminish and they need to be eaten soon.

Most of the carrots soups I have experienced feel like they are just pureed carrots with few other flavors. This one tastes complex and interesting, and it's hearty enough for a cold evening on the farm.

Carrot Soup

carrots, peeled, *1 ½ pounds (675 g)*
large onion, *1*
white potatoes, peeled, *½ pound (230 g)*
butter, *4 ounces (113 g)*
cream, *¾ cup (200 ml)*
beef stock, *1 quart (1 liter)*
salt, *to taste*
pepper, *to taste*

Peel all the vegetables, then dice the carrots and potatoes and slice the onion thinly. Set the skinned potatoes aside in a bowl, covered with water, until they are needed.

Melt butter over low heat in large sauté pan. Add onions and cook them till tender (about ten minutes). Then throw in carrots and cook until they slightly caramelize.

In a large soup pot, bring beef stock to a boil before adding the sautéed carrots and onions. Remove potatoes from soaking water and add to soup pot before bringing it back to a slow, slight boil. Cover and lower the heat, allowing the soup to simmer for 30 minutes.

Remove from the heat and puree with stem blender. Add cream and season to taste.

YIELD: *Makes enough for four people.*

JANUARY

January.

I am up at 6:30 this morning, late by summer standards, but amply early for the first day of January. After a few slow minutes, I open the front door of the Loghouse. The moon is still out and it looks like snow covering the ground. For that brief moment, I despair over the possibility of snow. Quickly, I realize that it is just cool, grey moonlight, a beautiful and a welcome relief.

After the short walk into the kitchen, I reach for the lights. The Cookhouse is full of light but looking out the windows, the moonlight disappears and all I see is the dismal, bright reflection: it looks so very dark out there. I put the kettle on and grind the beans for coffee. At 7:00, Mario comes in and gets bundled up to go out and milk the cows. We say nothing to each other. We have done this so many mornings. He sits and waits for it to be lighter out. And then, in a few minutes, I can hear the milking equipment in the parlor. The vacuum pump, whirling steadily.

I remain inside and drink my coffee. It's exceptionally quiet at this hour. I can hear the vacuum pump but little else. After Mario has completed the milking, I head out to check on the cows. The temperature dropped quickly last night after a few weeks of mild winter weather. The stock tanks are frozen. We didn't even bother to put floating heaters in them; there was no need.

The sun has crested the horizon and is now caught in the empty tree branches. It lights up the tops of the trees on the hill and then, eventually, whole trees before it passes over the tree tips. This winter morning, just a few days past the solstice, the sun is bright but so very low.

The frost-free water pipes in the pasture are frozen. They are designed so the water will drop down below grade whenever the valve is closed, but they were left ever so slightly on and now they are filled with frozen water. The long hoses lying across the pasture are equally frozen. Mario and I work to get them all in order to

refill the stock tanks for the cows now busily eating the hay Mario put out. Slowly, the water dribbles out of the long hoses to the water tanks and then, after a few minutes, it runs a bit faster as the long-frozen hoses defrost. Mario breaks the ice in the stock tanks and large shards of glass-like ice scatter. It looks like a crime has taken place up here on this quiet pasture where the only sound is a dozen cows chewing on brittle alfalfa hay. Today's glorious weather makes it a challenge to water the cows and laying hens and wash down the milking parlor, but compared to the past two weeks of rain and gloom and darkness, it is a joy. Slowly, the puddles of water have started receding from the pastures.

I leave Mario to finish while the sun is up but still not overhead. When he comes back to the kitchen, he is breathing deeply. He can't get used to the climate here compared to the Honduras, his birthplace. It is difficult to convince him that spring will arrive during these endless weeks of rain and cold.

I investigate the cooler. It feels fitting to begin a new year by cleaning out the cooler. As this is a dairy farm, there is always milk and cream and cheese in various forms and ages, hiding in the back of the box. I find old cream; soured cream. A perfect excuse to make a sour cream dough, roll it into a rectangle, and then make cinnamon rolls. Just a yeasty dough with some butter and sugar. The addition of a bit of cinnamon and the raisins I dried this fall will make them superb. I expect they will pull apart nicely and be just enough to make this morning more pleasurable.

Cinnamon Rolls

SOUR CREAM DOUGH
sour cream or crème fraîche, *2 cups (475 ml)*
sugar, *¼ cup (50 g)*
eggs, *2*
active dry yeast, *1 tablespoon (15 g)*
warm milk, *½ cup (120 ml)*
all-purpose flour, *5 cups (620 g)*

FILLING
butter, melted, *2 tablespoons (30 g)*
cinnamon, *1 tablespoon (15 g)*
raisins, *¾ cup (110 g)*
brown sugar, *3 tablespoons (35 g)*

Preheat oven to 350°F (175°C).

Mix sour cream, sugar, and eggs until well incorporated. Allow yeast to proof in warm milk with a touch of sugar for a few minutes. Combine proofed milk with sweetened sour cream and egg mixture. Slowly add flour, mixing until completely incorporated. Dough will remain stick and wet.

Refrigerate dough covered for a couple of hours to let rest and chill. Scrape dough onto floured board and roll into rectangle, ten inches by twenty. Spread butter, raisins and cinnamon over the surface and roll dough from the long end until a tube is formed. Cut tube into ten equal slices and place them swirl side down in a buttered baking dish. Leave in warm place for a couple of hours or until fully proofed.

Bake until browned and dough fully cooked through. I dab a bit of butter on top after they are baked.

YIELD: *Ten rolls.*

As I finish eating the cinnamon rolls, the sun starts to drop down again. It hits the sides of the birches on the hill. They blaze with the deep sunset light. It has been a mighty short bit of daylight. Mario eats the last of his cinnamon roll and heads out to the barn for the afternoon milking. Tim is nearly done making cheese for the day; soon I will hear him drive out. The side of the concrete creamery building is tinted by the deep orange sunset.

Daisy sits next to the concrete, feeling the heat, the only warm spot on the farm today. She knows where to feel the warmth of the sun.

Once the sun goes down and the farm is covered in darkness, other beasts become apparent. The cows are now in the upper pastures, out of my sight. Owls can be heard in the early part of the dark evening. Barred owls, I believe. Their call is "who cooks for you, who cooks for you?" I love this. Even though I have never actually seen them, I hear them and I want to believe this is what they are saying.

I walk back to the creamery to flip the cheeses that were made this afternoon, relying on the feel of concrete under my feet to find my way. Clouds have obscured the night's clear moon. When I get to the door of the cheese room, I can feel the heat escaping. The room is humid from the cheese making and the heaters were set

high. It is a stark contrast to the crisp air outside, and I wonder if raccoons and deer watch me from the shadows. It is so very dark this evening. In the past, one of my dogs would have accompanied me out to the cheese room. Tonight and for many other nights during the past few months, it has just been me.

Earlier that day, my dog, Daisy, was coughing up blood and having a difficult time breathing. In the last few weeks, she would fall over unexpectedly, as if her back legs were less connected to her body. But she still had good days, good times. She could rally and march up the hill, heading to the upper pasture to check on the cows with me. But today I knew she couldn't live much longer, so I texted the mobile veterinarian, Kiya, to come and take a look. I was still hopeful Daisy would live for a few more weeks.

I got Daisy sixteen years ago as a puppy from the Animal Control in Seattle. She was lithe and spirited and beautiful: a black cattle dog with a brindled white-and-black chest and a white-tipped tail. I loved this dog and she rarely left my side for the many years I commuted from the farm into the restaurant, and then she traveled with me in my truck to deliver milk and cheese. Only in the past two years did she stop commuting with me, spending her days exclusively on the farm. It was a remarkable sixteen years of farm life.

After she arrives, Kiya gently informs me that Daisy was not breathing well at all; she was suffocating and would not live long. She wants me to make the decision to put her down. She is obligated to have me decide. After a few questions, while Daisy stands there, sides precariously heaving in and out, trying to get air, I decide that she will die right then. I know it and I don't know it. It takes a while for the reality to get from my head to my heart. I feel relieved when I tell Kiya yes.

She goes out to her car to get two syringes and a hair shaver. It is a short walk from the Cookhouse to the parking lot, but it takes far longer for her to return than I thought possible. Daisy seemed to be dying rapidly in those three, four, five minutes. I feel awkward and alone with my companion of a decade and a half.

After she returns, she tells me what she will do. And asks me to write a check before. She has done this many times. She will leave quickly when she is done. She gives Daisy a heavy sedative that seems to take a long time to take effect. Slowly, Daisy lies down. Her breathing sounds healthy and for a moment, I think she might recover. Then she lays her head down and curiously licks her nose, again and again. Kiya shaves a bit of fur from her back leg and administers the second syringe. It is very quick.

There is no dramatic change. I close her eyes. They open up again when I pet her, so I close them again. Her perky ears stay up. I can't think she is dead. She just looks calm. Kiya checks her heart with a stethoscope and then gets up, putting her hand on my shoulder as she leaves, saying something I can't remember. It fills the space, though, in a nice way.

I start crying, my nose dripping incessantly onto the carpet. I sit on the carpet with Daisy for a few minutes and then decide to proceed. I find an old lab coat in the cheese room. It was made from white, strange polyester, but it will work. I just lay it over her, and then go to the shed to get a wheelbarrow and shovel so I can dig a hole. It is a gloomy winter day. A day of grief. How could I be this sad if this were the fourth of July?

The hole I dig fills partly with water from all the rains. I take the wheelbarrow and open the double doors of the Cookhouse so I could wheel it into the room. The wheelbarrow is huge and bright blue and it looks so very out of place in that room. And then I stop. The doors are wide open and the temperature is dropping. My instinct is to close the doors quickly, but I don't. Cold feels better. I pull up a chair and sit there, staring at the dusty lab coat covering my dear friend of a dog, her tail sticking out the bottom. It is easy to think she's just sleeping. I sit for a while. Sitting shiva. How could someone sit still for hours honoring the dead? I feel so anxious.

I get up, then sit down, then get up again. I have to pick her up and put her in the too-big wheelbarrow. I head out the Cookhouse to the milking parlor to get Mario to help me. I can hear the vacuum pump running; he is milking the cows. I am nearly to the closed door of the parlor before I stop and turn around. I don't want his help. I want to do this myself. But I don't want to do it.

I return to the cookhouse and sit again, then pace, then stand and then finally lean down and gently, lightly wrap Daisy's dead body with the lab coat. The entire tableau is funny looking. Kind of like gift wrapping her, but not at all.

Then I try to pick her up. She is floppy. No rigor mortis yet. Kiya drove away a half hour ago, forty-five minutes ago. An hour ago?

I head out the Cookhouse to the wet grave. In the intervening minutes, more water has streamed in. I have done this before with Byron and Spike. And that other dog, from years past, whose name I never remember. The hardest part is here. The sound as Daisy's body drops into the bottom of the hole in the ground. It hits the water and splashes a bit. Sounds bad. Not solemn or sad or reverential, just bad. Then the second worst part begins: putting the first couple shovelfuls of dirt on top of my much-loved companion of so many years. Doing so feels cruel and disrespectful and wrong, even if it is necessary. Eventually there is enough dirt in the hole and I am now just filling it in. Like planting a tree. Yes, it is like planting a tree. I am not crying anymore, although I still feel tight and sad.

I reach down for the large clods of sod-covered soil that I saved for the top. The shovel doesn't work well for this. I pick them up and arrange them over the fresh dirt to make it look like it did an hour ago, before Kiya pulled up, when Daisy was sitting on the rug in the kitchen, sleeping, and when things seemed so easy today. Before I put down my dog.

The mud on my hands feels like mourning. It gives me a connection to my buried dog. The earth. The wet mud. She is here in the ground. The ground where I grow pasture for the cows. And vegetables and fruits and trees on this farm. I will miss this dear, dear dog.

Once I finish and take a long walk, darkness has settled over the farm. I return to the Cookhouse and do what I know how to do: cook. I need to eat and making food calms me down and connects me to the past, to safe, happy times.

An omelet is what I decide to make. I once heard Ruth Reichl made omelets after she was fired from *Gourmet*. And at the end of the movie *Big Night*, when they are soon to lose their beautiful restaurant, Secondo cooks up some eggs in the quiet kitchen. It is the best scene in the entire movie. Quiet. Silent. Still. Just three guys in a kitchen as Stanley Tucci stirs some eggs in a pan.

Eggs heal.

I pull out my favorite French steel pan. From the cooler, I grab some lard, some fresh, slightly salty and slightly tart Flora's cheese, and some salmon that my neighbor smoked. He over-smoked it but it still tastes good.

After the flame has been on for a bit, the lump of lard quickly melts in the thick steel pan. Then I crack and whisk the eggs. I found them in the sink, at the end of the kitchen. Mario pulled them from the chicken coop a couple of hours ago, but he never cleaned them. It was a muddy, wet day, and the eggs are muddy too. Shitty. I clean them, but not very thoroughly since they are just for me. The egg spatters when it hits the hot, melted lard and quickly begins cooking. I like how the thin edges of egg whites can crisp up and tonight, I let them. Then I stir them a bit and get some egg under the cooked center before I pile on the cheese and the salmon I flaked with a fork, and put it in the hot oven. I have made many omelets over the years by myself while drunk or hungover or, like today, very sad and lonely.

After a quick minute in the hot gas oven, I take the steel pan out. The cheese has melted and the omelet's edges are beautifully crispy and brown. It rolls beautifully out from the pan onto the plate. The pan's black, steel surface is slick from thirty years of use

I eat it standing up at the stove, just like in *Big Night*. Tears run down my cheeks. I realize that I am standing on some bits of cheese that I dropped. There is no dog to eat it up.

I thought the hard part was putting Daisy down, but the hard part is the next day and the next day. It is coming home and finding the house empty. It is waiting for her to scratch at the door to get let in, only to never hear her; it is knowing I will never again step over her as she sleeps in the kitchen or call for her to come into the Loghouse. It is so very quiet. At night, I hear something and I can't simply think that it is her downstairs. I have to think about what it could be, what it might be.

The farm is still, soulless, lifeless.

I think it is time to bake.

I started my self-employed career thirty years ago, when I opened a tiny coffee shop in a neglected part of downtown Seattle. I was full of great optimism and felt that the world would flock to my ten-foot-wide café with its ten seats. In reality, I was not particularly experienced at either brewing coffee or baking breakfast pas-

Buttermilk Biscuits

8 Cups Flour - Sifted
2 T. Sugar
2 T. Baking Powder
1 t. Baking Soda

1 Pound Butter
3 1/2 Cups Buttermilk

Bread Dough

4 Cups Warm Water
6 T. (1/3 Cup) Sugar
2 T. Salt
4 T. Yeast

10 Cups Bread Flour

Proof yeast in water, salt and sugar in large mixer bowl.
With dough hook add flour.
Bring together and knead until smooth.

3 c.
4 T.
1·5 T.
3 T. Yeast
2.5 c.

2 cups / 1 cup

Sweet Dough

2 Cups Hot Milk
1/2 Pound Butter
1/2 Cup Sugar
2 T. Yeast
Salt
4 Eggs
4 Cups All purpose Flour

Milk Butter, sugar and salt in Hot milk in Large mixer bowl.
Proof yeast in milk mixture.
With Dough hook, add eggs and flour.
Knead until smooth.

Brioche Dough

2 T. Molasses
2 T Cup Warm Water
2 T. Yeast

6 t Molasses
1 1/2 Cup WarmWater
3 T. Yeast

Cups Bread Flour
2 T. Sugar
2 T. Salt
1 Cup Butter
6 Eggs

9 Cups Bread Flour
3 T. Sugar
3 t Salt
1 1/2 Cup Butter
9 Eggs

(36)

tries, but there was ample time to learn as few, if any, customers found me during those first few months.

Only recently did I find my original recipe book from those early days. It is a photo album with plastic pages where it was assumed someone would slip in snapshots. I filled the book with printed recipes, some typed on an old manual typewriter I kept from college until, a year or two later, I invested in a then-revolutionary personal computer and printed them out on a dot matrix printer.

The plastic pages are still caked with flour and egg and sugar, and the ink is rather faded but I can read them all and have begun baking from this time capsule. When I flip through these pages, I remember those days. I was in my mid-twenties and full of hope, yet had no idea what the future would bring.

Baking settles me. Making a batch of scones or biscuits takes me right back to those simple days, getting up at four in the morning and walking the block and a half from my tiny downtown apartment to the shop and then baking for three hours before I opened the door and began serving coffee and freshly baked pastries to the neighborhood.

The farm is so very quiet now, without my dog. Without any dog. I save a bit of milk for her from cleaning the bulk tank in the milk room, even though she is nowhere to be found.

I think about the role of animals here on this farm. I have slaughtered many over the years: too many chickens to count, at least a couple dozen pigs, and perhaps three or four mature cows and a couple of young steers. I can completely detach from the process, which is appropriate. There is a wall between me and death because I have raised these animals for their meat, for their sustenance, and death is a part of that process. When I defend eating meat, I say this. I contend that you should never mix up your pet with a farm animal. Your only experience is with a dog or a cat. My cows, my pigs, are not my pets. And yet this week I have killed my dog, and watched her die on my kitchen floor.

My emotions today are different than any I have from shooting a bullet into the head of a pig or a cow, always between the eyes but just a bit off center to miss the thick part of the skull. I have done it well so many times. And yet there I was, kneeling on the red, Persian carpet as Daisy slowly went limp onto that rug. Death is not all the same here on the farm.

Buttermilk Biscuits

all-purpose flour, *8 cups (960 g)*
sugar, *2 tablespoons (30 g)*
baking powder, *2 tablespoons (30 g)*
baking soda, *1 teaspoon (5 g)*
butter, *1 pound (450 g)*
buttermilk, *3 ½ cups (820 ml)*

Pre-heat oven to 375°F (190°C).

In mixing bowl, sift together dry ingredients. Chop butter into small slices. Smear butter into flour mixture. Slowly add buttermilk until it is slightly incorporated. Dump mixing bowl contents onto counter and gently pat it into an inch thick rectangle. Cut into 2-inch rounds.

Bake on a thick baking sheet until brown (about fifteen minutes).

YIELD: *Ten biscuits.*

————————————

The first cuts of beef that get pulled from the freezer are the fancy ones: the rib eyes and the tenderloins. They are easy to cook and fun to serve at a party. Traditionally I serve large steaks for my birthday. I drag up bottles of red wine from the cheese cave, cook some steaks, and finish the meal with a cake or pie or both. I am most fortunate my birthday is the middle of June. I couldn't bear to have a birthday fete in the dead of winter.

Yesterday I pulled up three odd packages from the freezer and left them to defrost in the refrigerator. I knew they would be tasty but it would take much more effort to capture their beefy essence. This morning, I unwrap the beef and spread it out on the cutting table. They are strange cuts, full of sinew and silver skin, but still very useable. Little by little, I trim the beef from the inedible parts with a generous hand. In a few minutes' time, I have a pile of nice two-inch cubes of beef and a nearly equal pile of gristle.

And then I put two pots on the stove: a medium stockpot with a heavy bottom and a large Le Creuset braiser. Into each, I spoon a large lump of lard and turn the flame on high. Into the stockpot go the lesser bits; into the braiser, half of the best meats. Both sputter and pop as the meat hits the hot lard. The goal for both these pots is the same at this point: to brown the beef and get the best possible crusty base for flavor. I only put in half the beef chunks at a time to keep the steam down and the browning at its best. All of the lesser bits, I just dump in. Over the course of twenty minutes, I stand at the stove and move the beef around, getting all the edges brown and crusty and caramelized. The smell is in the kitchen is heady and rich.

When the bits are browned throughout, I add three quarts of water and begin to make stock. Once it comes up to a boil, I lower the flame and let it simmer, full but not crazy. On the other burner, I turn the flame off and let the braiser rest for a few minutes. After three quarters of an hour, the stock has begun to capture enough of the flavor that I can start. I relight the braised beef and bring it up to high heat. The beef crackles, almost like it is about to burn. I grab a ladle and pull a half a cup of the early stock and pour it over the beef. It steams and sputters and after three or four ladlesful, it calms down and begins to boil. With a wooden spoon, I pull up the bits stuck to the bottom and sides of the heavy cast iron pot and the dish just gets more flavorful.

I keep braising the beef in the heavy open pot while slowly simmering stock in the high stockpot. The dance goes on, more water in the second, more stock added to the first. I take a break, covering the braiser and putting it in the oven to slowly finish and pushing the stockpot to the rear of the range to simmer on a very low heat.

And then I begin a third pot: a thick copper pot half filled with water and milk. I bring the watery milk to a slow boil and then gently pour in a couple of cups of polenta, stirring all the while. After ten or fifteen minutes, it will absorb most of the liquid, and is begging for more. Then that same ladle will grab some beef stock and add it to the nearly cooked polenta. As those beef bits cook, they will start to fall apart and small bits of beef will be added to the cornmeal, making it even richer. The beef is nearly braised, starting to fall apart as well.

In a few more minutes, the polenta is cooked through and the gritty bits have broken down and become smooth and comforting. I spoon it into large, shallow bowls and add a nice bit of braised beef from the oven and a spoonful of the still-simmering stock from the back of the stove.

Beef Polenta

whole milk, *1 cup (240 ml)*
water, *as needed*
polenta, dried, ground corn, *1 cup (170 g)*
beef stock, *2 cups (480 ml)*
salt, *to taste*
pepper, *to taste*

Bring milk and one cup of water to a simmer in a two-quart saucepot. Add polenta, stirring continuously. Allow to simmer while stirring. Add hot beef stock by the ladleful, as needed, until polenta is fully cooked (in approximately fifteen minutes). Season with salt and pepper. Serve in warm, low bowls with braised beef and dress with reduced beef stock.

YIELD: *Makes enough for two.*

FEBRUARY

February.

Geographically speaking, Vashon Island is a peculiar place. Just off of Seattle, separated by water from the city and only accessible by ferry, it is both rural and completely suburban. From my upper pasture, it feels as though I am in the wilderness, trees as far as I can see, and then I walk down my driveway and I am surrounded by houses and yards identical to the sprawl found throughout the nation. Once I reach the main road, I often must wait for the steady stream of cars to subside before I can drive out of the farm and head to the nearby town with its expansive parking lots and big box-style stores. At times, I love the distinctly modern feel of the island and at others, I hide away on my pastures with my cows and pretend I am living hours out from the city and all its trappings. And yet, if I could climb to the top of the tallest tree on the upper pasture, I think I could peer over the island and see the skyline of Seattle, a thoroughly modern city, minutes away.

Almost every year, I have the opportunity to feel the more wild aspect of this suburban island when the power goes out. Vashon has many trees and long power lines that fall victim to the weighty snow and deep winds of winter. This February day is not unusual: I awake to find the farm blanketed in wet snow. The beauty of this scene is quickly disrupted as I realize that the power has gone down. This, sadly, does not mean I have a moment to relax but instead that I must quickly help Mario get the generator hooked up to run the vacuum pump in the milking parlor. Even though it happens every year, we are always taken aback and have to scramble to find the small generator and the gas tanks and the extension cords. Some year we will be better prepared, but today we are both searching for a long electric cord.

Cows are magnificent creatures of habit. They are easy to manage because they follow the same pattern every day. They know when to come into the lower paddock and then to the parlor, where they line up and one by one walk in to be milked and fed. However, any change to their routine is extremely disruptive to them and they immediately balk, spending their energy investigating the changes and deciding if they approve, which they generally do not. The sound of the generator is a disturbance that they find unacceptable. Through trial-and-error during past power outages, we now place the gas-fired generator on the far side of the creamery and run a long extension cord up to the vacuum pump in the attic of the parlor. The cows approve of this system and will file into the parlor despite the bright orange cord hanging where they can see it.

Once we have this system set up and fully operational, the morning looks like any other. The cows are milked and fed and then returned to the barn. The generator is switched to the bulk tank and the milk is fully chilled and held for making cheese the next day. And then Mario drives down the long driveway through the snow and I am left with the farm. And the quiet.

The day is extraordinary. The sunlight reflects off of the fresh white snow, filling the kitchen with a bright, even glow, full but not harsh in any way. Summer sunshine is never like this; neither is dreary winter light. This is a special light, mostly for its rarity but also for the glow after weeks of low winter illumination.

But it is the quiet that I relish. The farm isn't particularly noisy in general, but there are a lot of modern sounds that keep the creamery operating. A bank of coolers stand on one wall of the Cookhouse, some filled with aging cheeses, another with food for the kitchen. The compressors run on and off throughout the day, their fans humming incessantly. The high-temperature dishwasher is run many times, the forceful pump rinsing and cleaning for hours, sanitizing the cheese molds and tools of cheese making. And the boiler that heats the Cookhouse and Loghouse is always heating and pumping warm water through the floors, clicking as it changes cycles with regularity. It is not a noisy place but it isn't silent. Except for today.

All the motors are stalled, the compressors stopped, the pumps idle, and it is glorious. Perhaps there are always birds loudly chirping in the winter months but they seem to have come alive today. A walk around the farm, slowed by the deep snow, is filled with their chirping, chatting with each other, calling out for responses. The birds have the stage today; it is their day to fill the air with their sounds.

There is little to do today. No cheese can be made, and there is no cleaning to do. The employees have left. It is just me in the kitchen. Thankfully I have a gas range and can cook what I have on hand. I could conceivably walk to town or even

drive the farm truck up to see if the grocery story is open. I know they have large generators that run their enterprise no matter the weather or circumstance, but I decide to be in this moment, this all-day or maybe multiple- day experience, of quiet and calm.

For the first hour, it is distracting. When I open the refrigerator, nothing happens: no light goes on, no fan blows. A few things sit on the shelves and stare back at me. And then I get used to it and enjoy it. I find a book, Hemingway, and sit on the long bench and read and eat an omelet with tomato chutney left over from Thanksgiving dinner. I consciously leave my phone aside. It is almost dead, little power left. I could sit in my car and charge it there, but why? This is a treat: no calls, no texts, no Instagram. Nothing to distract from the even light and the quiet. It is a day of conscious uncoupling, if you will. It is so very difficult to do it on a regular day. We are pulled into the modern world daily and held there with a firm grip. But today that is all left behind. It is Hemingway and eggs and chutney. It is easy to read, flipping the pages steadily with no interruptions, as if it is 1979 again. Back to a time when things moved slowly and an afternoon with a good book was commonplace.

As the afternoon progresses, the temperature begins to drop in the kitchen. The boiler has been off for hours now. The environment is slowly seeping in and I am closer and closer to the world outside the delicate windows. It feels real.

I interrupt the Hemingway with walks over to the rack holding the many jars of summer canning, the pickles and jams and jellies and chutneys and sauces. The glass jars each reveal a different season and time on the farm. I finish the bit of left-over tomato chutney and start on a fresh jar, enjoying it tremendously. I open some applesauce and it was the most beautiful applesauce I had ever had. I keep a small stack of dried pears next to my book and nibble on them with delight while flipping pages. Everything was better and more flavorful and sharper and brighter. It was as if my senses could concentrate on the food and not be overwhelmed by the noise and complexity of our modern life.

Perhaps it was just being calm and in the moment, present, but I made a great decision: less jam and more chutney. Raspberry jam, blackberry jam, and the rest are great, really great. There is just too much. However, there is never enough chutney. I could finish a quart of well-made chutney by eating it right out of the Mason jar with a spoon. This summer, I will try to avoid the jam making; I only need a small amount.

Mario returned, started up the generator again, and quickly milked the cows, eager to finish and return home. It was a brief interruption but the creamery is far enough away that the generator didn't break my enjoyment. The farm was quiet once again as the sun sat low in the horizon, the temperature dropping as nighttime began to take hold. And then, just as unexpectedly as it had gone out, the power returned. The coolers kicked in and the boiler fired up and the lights came on. Sadly, the calm ended and I was completely complicit, plugging my phone back in, eager to check for emails and texts and visits and likes and Instagram and the all the other parts of my modern life. It is a powerful pull and yet one that could be resisted for one day. It took a layer of deep white snow to do it.

———————————

February begins the push to clear the larder of the prior year's harvests. There is still garlic, a few onions that have sprouted, some firm shallots, and boxes of potatoes eager to begin their next phase of life. The shallots will make it until summer, I expect. The garlic is in a rapid decline towards a dried death and the onions will soon be compost. But the race is on to utilize as many potatoes as possible before they are lost.

A favorite use of mine is the gratin dauphinois, primarily on the account that it helps to use up those last cloves of garlic as well as the potatoes, and because high quality, rich milk is always in abundance at this dairy farm. We make the least amount of cheese and ice cream during this time of year; many of the cows are dry in this slow period. In a few weeks' time, they will have their calves, freshen, and produce the prodigious amounts of milk needed for the warm weather ice cream season. But in February, we can always give up a bit of milk for a hearty gratin.

As you might imagine, I have friends who love food. Maybe they are great cooks, perhaps great gardeners or farmers or just love a delicious meal. I tend to surround myself with those who find food and eating integral to their life. I do have one friend, however, who may perhaps be more opinionated about food than I.

Ian lives in Europe but is from Chicago and came out to stay at the farm with me so we could cook and eat and cook some more. I am used to being able to direct my own kitchen. In this case, I was unable to master such command. Hours after his arrival, we had a serious conflict about chicken legs and pasta. Cuts of meat and types of wine can bring us to verbal fisticuffs, always followed up by a sumptuous meal.

Gratin dauphinois was a special challenge. Ian had lived in Paris while in school, as had I—albeit three decades apart—and was well versed in the intricacies of the gratin. I too held my ideas about the potato dish. After much wrangling, we agreed to disagree. He believes a gratin dauphinois has cheese throughout the layers of potatoes; I believe in a purer dish of potatoes, milk, cream, and butter. We are different guys.

We found the best solution for dinner that evening was to each make our own version and to serve both to our guests. I would say we both enjoyed the other's version, but there was little chance of ever changing our deeply held beliefs about the proper gratin.

This is my favorite kind of recipe. It can be done with great care and time, slowly and methodically layering the potatoes in concentric circles to create a masterpiece of potatoes or, more likely, as a quick side dish. There have been occasions when I thought I had much more time and suddenly realized how late it was and that guests were soon to arrive. I can run a few potatoes through the mandolin in record time, splaying them out and covering them with milk as the cars are pulling up the driveway. By the time we finish a glass of wine and the roast is ready, with luck, the gratin will be beautiful, golden and bubbly.

It's a funny recipe. I really don't want to even write the quantities. It depends on the potatoes. And the dimensions of the dish. And whether you are silly enough to take Ian's recommendation and load it with cheese. Too much milk and cream and it will never cook and be a mushy—but tasty—mess. Too little milk and cream and it will become dry and hard before the potatoes cook. Load the gratin dish with the potatoes and then pour the liquid in until it just about comes to the top of the potatoes. Not quite the top but very close. It should take about an hour to bake. And always put it on the middle shelf; it needs the reflective heat to brown the top.

Gratin Dauphinois

potatoes, *2 pounds (900 g)*
garlic clove, *1*
butter, *2 tablespoons (30 g)*
cheese, grated, *⅓ pound (35 g), optional*
salt, *to taste*
pepper, *to taste*
milk, *¾ cup (180 ml)*
cream, *¼ cup (60 ml)*

Pre-heat oven to 375°F (190°C).

Peel and thinly slice potatoes; keep submerged in water if you are not ready to use them immediately.

Rub a shallow 11" by 9" (28 cm by 23 cm) gratin dish with cut clove of garlic, then thoroughly coat surface with butter. Chop garlic clove and reserve. Layer sliced potatoes in concentric circle in base of gratin dish, overlapping each piece. After each layer, add grated cheese (if desired), salt, and pepper. Utilize all the potato slices, making three layers.

Add grated cheese to top layer. Pour in milk and cream along with salt, pepper, and remaining chopped garlic.

Bake in center of oven for one hour or until potatoes are cooked through.

This gratin is a frequent meal for me when alone on a winter night at the farm. It is rich and filling and warming. A better use would be as a side dish to an equally French main course of boeuf bourguignon. When the cow was slaughtered weeks ago, I made sure to have Lauren include stew meat in two-pound packages.

Boeuf Bourguignon

beef chuck, trimmed and cut into 1-inch cubes, *2 ½ pounds (1.3 kg)*
lard, *5 tablespoons (75 g)*
all-purpose flour, *⅓ cup (40 g)*
salt, *2 teaspoons (10 g)*
pepper, *2 teaspoons (10 g)*
carrots, peeled and large dice, *4 medium*
garlic cloves, finely diced, *2*
red wine, *1 ½ cups (350 ml)*
beef stock, *1 ½ cups (350 ml)*
onion, peeled and large dice, *1 large or 2 medium*

Preheat oven to 325°F (165°C).

Trim beef chuck and cut it into 1-inch cubes.

In a large, heavy cast iron pot, melt 3 tablespoons (45 g) lard and allow to heat over medium high heat. Season flour with salt and pepper, then dust it over the beef. Add beef to pot and allow it to brown, scraping bits as it cooks, ten minutes. Once fully browned, lower heat.

Peel and large dice carrots. Chop onions and garlic. In a separate saucepan over medium high heat, melt remaining lard and sauté carrots, garlic, and onions. When onions are translucent and carrots beginning to cook (ten minutes) add them to beef pot and stir to combine.

In the same saucepan used to saute vegetables, combine red wine and beef stock and bring to a simmer on medium heat. Add this wine and stock mixture to the beef and vegetables and stir, scraping up the browned bits on the bottom and sides of the pot. Cover and cook slowly in oven. Test for doneness by piercing a large piece of beef with a wooden spoon: if it breaks easily, it is fully cooked and the beef is tender. This takes approximately two hours.

Serve with gratin dauphinoise.

YIELD: *Enough for four hearty souls in the deep of winter.*

Ian felt I wasn't eating enough vegetables and insisted on preparing more vegetables. Thankfully he had brought this recipe from the Netherlands. I am familiar with cooking cabbage with butter and garlic and thyme but the beef broth and cream make it special and hearty and ideal to accompany the gratin and the beef.

Creamed Cabbage

savoy or other green cabbage, medium size, *1*
butter, *4 tablespoons (60 g)*
garlic cloves, *1 ½*
thyme, fresh, *1 ½ teaspoons (25 g)*
beef broth, *1 cup (240 ml)*
cream, *¾ cup (180 ml)*
salt, *to taste*
pepper, *to taste*

Cut cabbage into slices roughly ½" (1 cm) wide.

Melt the butter with garlic and thyme in a large, heavy-bottomed saucepan. When garlic is cooked but not burned, add cabbage in batches. As first batch of cabbage begins to sweat and cook, continue adding cabbage until it is all in the pan, then stir frequently. The cabbage should begin to soften on low heat. Add beef broth and bring to a boil, then lower the heat and let the broth simmer for ten minutes. Add the cream and continue to simmer until cabbage is tender and cooked through. Season with salt and pepper to taste.

The larder is still filled with many jars of alcohol soaked fruits. There are a couple jars of raisins soaked in rum and despite the cold weather here, I am compelled to make a batch of rum raisin ice cream. I start with a standard base recipe and then, when the ice cream is not quite frozen, fold in the rum soaked raisins. Do try and abstain from adding vanilla extract. Although very tasty, it is such a common ploy and with great milk, cream, and eggs, the flavor of the ice cream should suffice.

Rum Raisin Ice Cream

egg yolks, *6*
organic cane sugar, *1 ¼ cups (250 g)*
tapioca starch, *4 tablespoons (60 g)*
salt, *pinch*
whole milk, *3 cups (700 ml)*
cream (30%), *3 cups (700 ml)*
raisins soaked in rum, drained, *1 ½ cups (225 g)*

Whisk yolks and sugar together, then add tapioca starch, a pinch of salt and ½ cup milk in a large mixing bowl.

Warm remaining milk and cream in large sauce pan. When warm but not simmering, pour milk into egg mixture in a stream, whisking to fully incorporate.

Pour complete mixture back into saucepan and continue to cook over medium heat. Do not allow to simmer, but cook until sauce thickens slightly.

Pour into mixing bowl through a sieve to strain out bits of egg, then cover and chill overnight.

Add base to ice cream churn and freeze as usual. When nearly frozen, add the raisins, folding them in with a rubber spatula until fully incorporated.

YIELD: *2 quarts.*

MARCH

March.

I never thought my son would be a twenty-three-year-old Honduran cow milker named Mario. Actually, I never really thought I would have a son. I am a single gay man in my mid-fifties with barely a romantic relationship in my half-century past. I always thought I would find a nice man, or a nice man would find me, and my life would resemble the lives of people around me: married with a kid or two.

But it never happened. Or it hasn't happened yet. The husband part at least. I think I now have the child I expected to have but never seemed to get.

He isn't who I expected in any way. He is twenty-three—certainly not a newborn or even a child by any stretch. I have only known him a few years, since the day he arrived at my dairy farm to fill in for a friend of his who wanted the day off. I looked out at the milking parlor and there he was, working with my cows, much to my surprise.

The next week, he worked a couple of shifts, milking the cows, cleaning out the barn, and feeding the pigs and chickens. His friend was happy to move on, taking a job more to his liking in construction. And little by little, he became my full-time cow milker. Now I see him every morning and afternoon, out in the milking parlor or driving the tractor up the hill to the pastures, moving the cows around the fresh grass. And in the process, he became a part, an unexpected part, of my life.

His life centers as much on this small farm as it does with his family, I would guess. He likes to work and loves this place. It is an easy place to love. There is always plenty of great food and it is quiet.

As the past couple years progressed, I realized I was getting rather attached to him. I wanted him to succeed and have a great life in his new country. He is honest and fair and kind. He is strikingly handsome, and charming and chatty when he feels comfortable; incredibly shy when he is not.

But I knew that I wasn't interested in him romantically at all, but rather as a son. I had long since given up on having children, thinking a single gay man would be a rather poor father. Or that I wouldn't have enough time.

But I have had many employees over three decades of being self-employed, and I have been friends with many of them. They are my family of sorts. But then he asked me for help and I knew this employee was different.

He needed to get a drivers license and I agreed to help him. It is a slightly complicated process: going to the Department of Motor Vehicles, filling out the paperwork, taking the tests, and so on. I really didn't have an idea of how it would go until I found myself in a large, crowded hall, waiting for his number to be announced. It felt good to be there with him. I know this culture well and could easily navigate it for him. He quickly passed the written test and then we got an appointment for the practical driving test.

When we arrived and parked in the designated spot and patiently waited for the inspector to come out to the car, he was visibly nervous. His confidence collided with his dread of dealing with an imposing American official judging him. When I got out of the car and went to wait on the sidewalk while the inspector got in, I realized that my role as parent was clear. I wanted to so badly to get in the car with them, to help him along, to explain to the official that he has prepared, that he can drive well, that he is responsible. To protect him. To soften the blows for my young charge. I nervously paced the sidewalk during his ten-minute drive around the neighborhood. I watched everywhere for sight of the grey Toyota stopping, signaling, and turning on the adjacent streets. And then when he returned and the inspector got out of the car with a distinct frown on his face, I was devastated, and realized I needed to console the rejected Mario.

Driving back to the farm we endlessly discussed the difference between looking casually for oncoming traffic and making it obvious that he was indeed looking in every direction. "But I did look!" was all he could say. A couple of weeks later, we returned and I again found myself pacing back and forth, confident that he had heard my instructions to turn his head and look clearly. But when the second inspector got out of the car and came out to go over what was inadequate with me, it was clear that I was connected to my cow milker.

Thankfully, on our third attempt, he passed the driving test and received his license. He was thoroughly excited and proud and wanted me to know that he had succeeded although he still held onto the idea that the first two inspectors simply didn't like him. I had hoped for a great teaching moment, but alas, I had to settle with the lesson that perseverance pays off.

I had become a helicopter parent, coming so close to insisting that I ride in the car during the test. I wanted to protect him from the worries and anguish of taking the test. For years, I have been the middle-aged guy who would lecture anyone who would listen to me of the sad demise of proper parenting by those who took too active a role in their children's lives. The weird, sad, odd irony to this was that I wasn't parenting a twelve-year-old. And I wasn't even a parent. I was simply a farmer and cheesemaker with a charming employee to mentor. Or help to successfully receive a driver's license.

———————

His culinary tastes are unique, I would say, and rather refined for a young man. He insists on eating local, wood-fired bread exclusively, telling me of his great error in buying a commercially prepared loaf when the local boules were sold out. He swears he can only eat the aged tomme we produce here, and he does indeed eat it in great volume. Our Camembert-style cheese is not to his liking, however. I have been corrected many times that the culinary culture of Honduras and Mexico are distinctly different when I add chilies for spice to carne asada or begin to prepare a green salsa from tomatillos from the garden. But grilled meats are always to his enjoyment and although I think of it as a summer dish, grilling up some skirt steak in March is my way of pushing the seasons a bit, just enough to make me believe it will be summer soon and we can barbecue at the farm. Even smoking up the kitchen by cooking beef on the top of the range makes it feel a bit more like June than this rainy month. Springtime is just weeks away, I tell myself.

The greenhouse is a bit crowded these days. Around the sides are flats of seeds starting. Tomatoes and peppers on heated germination mats, slowly growing towards summer. Small pots of shallots and larger flats of onions have just left for the garden. Flats filled with small cubes of soil hold spring vegetables: broccoli, cabbage, kale, and the like.

In the corners are plants that live in the greenhouse permanently: lemon verbena and rose geranium, both planted to supply the ice cream shop with herbaceous ingredients early and late in the season when those herbs are unviable outside. The lemon verbena has come out of its winter hibernation but the rose geraniums appear dead, frozen to their core from the deep winter chills.

And in the center of the greenhouse is a large stock tank: an ovoid, steel tank that would normally hold water for the cows. This one has long since rusted out so we use to raise baby chicks. A single, red heat lamp hangs from the framework of the greenhouse down to a foot above the floor of the tank, warming tiny bits of fluff and feather. The chicks scurry around their large pen when I enter to check on the seedlings, and chirp loudly as I leave. In a few weeks' time, they will move onto the outside chicken coops and the seedlings will be robust plants in their individual pots, but this month is all about the start of the growing season.

There is a rite of spring that I enjoy. A necessary part of raising seedlings for the garden is thinning the overseeded pots and flats. It is easy to sprinkle too many seeds too close to each other, and the sprouts need to be isolated so they continue to grow properly before they are planted out in the garden. For years, I would just pull these errant fledglings and toss them aside onto the floor of the greenhouse. And then I realized that they were delightful, prescient bits of summer. And so now I collect them as I go and bring them into the kitchen. Collectively, they could barely be considered a salad but they still accent snacks well. They are, in the parlance of the trend trade, microgreens. I think of them as leftovers from the greenhouse. What is remarkable is that, even though they are just a few days old, they taste like the final vegetable: they have the spice of radishes, the greenness of broccoli, the bite of cabbage, and so on.

Toasted Hearty Bread with Fromage Blanc and Tiny Seedlings

multigrain bread, freshly baked, *1 loaf*
fromage blanc (see recipe)
microgreens / greenhouse gleanings

This is an easy recipe—hardly a recipe at all. There is a baker across the street from the farm who has a wood-fired oven and makes an excellent multi-grain bread. We slice it up, lightly toast it in the oven, and then spread on a thick layer of fromage blanc after the bread has cooled. A sprinkling of seedlings from the greenhouse finishes off this springtime snack.

Fromage blanc is a simple dairy preparation, part of our method of making cheese. It is a simple thing for us to pull a gallon of warm milk from the bat and add some cultures. In two days it becomes this delightful spread. Best on toast, but you will find many uses for it. As always, the quality of the milk is paramount. If you don't have a herd of Jersey cows feet from your kitchen, search out a great source of farm milk and use that.

FROMAGE BLANC
whole milk, *1 gallon (3.8 liters)*
Mesophile Aroma B culture, *.1 gram*
rennet, *.4 ml*

N.B. Both the culture and the rennet are available from online cheese making supply companies aimed at the home cheese maker.

Heat milk to 90°F (32°C) Use a kitchen thermometer to make sure it has heated to the proper temperature. Add culture and allow the milk to sit for 20 minutes. Then add rennet and store milk in a temperate place (65 – 72°F / 20 – 22°C) where it won't be disturbed. Let it set for 8 to 12 hours.

With a large scoop, gently move curd to a cheesecloth-lined strainer over another container. Sprinkle curd with 1 ½ tablespoons salt. Let it drain at room temp for 3 hours, then move to the refrigerator and allow it to continue draining for another 10 to 12 hours.

Press finished cheese through colander.

YIELD: *1 gallon (3.8 liters).*

At this time of year, especially if the weather has been poor, there is little fresh, new food in the gardens. Rhubarb is the great exception. Without fail, it emerges from the damp, cold earth and produces thick, rigid stalks of goodness. Odd that we have come to cultivate such an unusual plant, but it is divine and most welcome on the cusp of the long, wet winter.

There are myriad uses for rhubarb and my preferences change over the year. In elementary school, I won a speaking contest by demonstrating the making of *Rhubarb Delight*—the ingredient list included a box of cake mix and a box of cherry Jello—in addition to the rhubarb. I have stopped making this concoction, thankfully.

Ian brought a bottle of superb Dutch gin with him from the Netherlands, so a spring cocktail was in order. The sweetness and tartness of the rhubarb and the deep flavors of the gin make a great combination. The drink is also outrageously pink. It signals that spring is on the way, if only for the length of the cocktail.

Rhubarb Cocktail

gin, *4 fl oz (120 ml)*
rhubarb syrup, *4 fl oz (120 ml)*
tonic water, *8 fl oz (240 ml)*
ice

Combine gin and syrup in a couple tall cocktail glasses, add ice and top off with tonic water.

YIELD: *Makes drinks for 2.*

RHUBARB SYRUP
rhubarb, chopped, *¾ pound (340 g)*
water, *1 cup (240 ml)*
organic cane sugar, *½ cup (100 g)*

Cook rhubarb with water and sugar over medium heat until tender and completely softened (5 minutes). Put into sieve and allow to slowly drain into a bowl. Don't push it to speed the process. Just allow it to drip.

There are still a few errant potatoes left in the pantry, full of eyes that are beginning to sprout but still very much edible. These aren't the best potatoes for baking but they are perfect for gnocchi. The starches have started to break down, making for light gnocchi.

Soon potatoes will be planted in the garden, but these last bits of the last harvest need to be utilized.

Gnocchi

russet potatoes, *2 pounds (900 g)*
egg yolks, *3*
all-purpose flour, *1 cup (120 g)*
salt, *2 teaspoons (10 g)*
fresh herbs

Preheat oven to 350°F (175°C). Peel potatoes. Trim off ends and cut potatoes into ¾ inch thick wedges, about 1 ½ inches long. Try to make them symmetrical so they cook evenly when boiled. Place the cut potatoes into a pot of water. When finished, fill the pot with more water until all potatoes are just submerged. Boil them for about 15 minutes or until you can just piece them with a knife.

Remove potatoes with a straining spoon in order to keep the starch residue in the water. Rice the potatoes while still hot. Lay the riced potatoes onto a baking tray and cook in the oven for a few minutes so dry out a bit. Too long and they will taste roasted but a few minutes will allow them to steam and release some moisture.

Mix riced potatoes with the yolks, flour, and salt. Divide mixture into 4 parts. Roll each part into a 'rope' about the thickness of your thumb. Use a knife to cut into ⅓ inch (8 mm) thick pieces. As you cut them lay them out on a dusted sheet pan. Don't stack them at all and try to keep them from touching one another. As soon as the entire lot is cut, get them to the freezer to chill quickly. Store them in the freezer, dropping the frozen nuggets into generously salted boiling water to cook.

Boil the gnocchi for 3 – 4 minutes in gently boiling water. Once they float, remove gently with a straining ladle. Dress with melted butter and fresh herbs. Sage is

always the classic herb to accompany gnocchi but whatever is growing this time of year is ideal, I would say. The Italian parsley often reseeds well and begins to emerge early in the spring. The chives are always abundant if not terribly tender. Even cilantro peaks out from winter and could be added to the butter.

This recipe makes approximately 200 of these dear, plump gnocchi. Spread out on a sheet pan in the freezer they resemble a large package of those pastel colored marshmallows always used for hot chocolate, yet so much tastier. Make the full recipe, use half for meal and keep the rest in the freezer for the evening when there just isn't anything to make.

If you have made it this far into the first volume of this journal, I guess you have noticed I included few salads or vegetable recipes. I certainly enjoy both during the warmer summer months, but during dark winter I stick to more "meat and potatoes" cuisine. Little is harvested here during the cold months. Some years I am lucky and broccoli or cabbages make it through the wet autumn, but often little remains other than root vegetables. Then spring arrives and the first green bits appear.

Dandelion greens are the earliest greens to respond to the lengthening days of sunlight. If they are young and have grown quickly, they are bright and tasty with a hint of bitterness. If it has been a mild spring, the remnants of kale plants left from last fall will begin to sprout with new leaves. Even old cabbage stems might sprout new leaves.

This tomato vinaigrette is rich enough to coat the deep green leaves with flavor. It is a great use of the tomatoes we dried at the end of the summer, especially the cherry tomatoes. They are thin and easy to incorporate into the dressing. Larger, plumper sun-dried tomatoes could certainly work but they need to be finely chopped. This is one of the rare instances when I will buy olive oil from the store. I prefer to base my cuisine around the Jersey butter, pork lard, and beef tallow that is harvested here. Alas, none of those make for a great vinaigrette dressing.

Dried Tomato Dressing

dried tomatoes, chopped, *2 tablespoons (30 g)*
apple cider vinegar, *3 tablespoons (45 ml)*
olive oil, *6 tablespoons (90 ml)*
eggs, *2*
chives, *1 tablespoon (15 g)*
salt, *to taste*
pepper, *to taste*

Hard boil eggs for 10 minutes, then cool them in cold water. Peel the shells and separate the yolks from the whites. Discard the whites and crush the yolks with a fork.

Soften tomatoes in warm water for five minutes, then drain and discard water. While the tomatoes are softening, blend crushed egg yolks with vinegar. Add chives, tomatoes, and olive oil to yolk mixture.

Season to taste with salt and pepper.

YIELD: *Enough to dress a salad for four.*

———————

Thank you for coming with me on this trip through fall and winter on the farm. There were dark, cold, wet, and even snowy days, but the larder stayed filled with plenty of pickles, dried fruits, and potatoes, and the freezer was stuffed with ample beef, pork, and chicken, and of course a bag of ice for making cocktails. My dog Daisy died and a cow was slaughtered, but there was still joy and plenty of hearty meals with friends. I ate a great deal of beef and too many potato gratins, and I never stopped eating ice cream for dessert, but I love it and I am sure I will keep the same routine next winter. And soon spring will arrive and summer will follow, bringing with it tomatoes and basil and raspberries and long, pleasant dinners on the porch.

COLOPHON

Volume I of *Farm Food* was written and photographed by Kurt Timmermeister during the fall and winter of 2016–17 at Kurtwood Farms on Vashon Island, Washington. All photos were shot using a Hasselblad 500 V series camera on Kodak Porta 400 film and processed by Panda Labs in Seattle.

Cover and page design by Dan D Shafer. Copy editing was done by Neal Swain. Food editing and recipe development was done by Ian Barillas-McEntee.

The text is set in Arno, a font named for a river in Italy and inspired by Italian Rennaisance typefaces, designed by Roger Slimbach.

Printed and bound by Consolidated Press in Seattle, Washington.

PUBLISHED BY COOKHOUSE PUBLISHING

FIRST PRINTING, 2500 COPIES